Dear John,

I hope you enjoy "Maestro" and share the inspiration

Messages

Eric J. Giglione

To my daughter Nicole

Foreword

Messages is the essence of what I learned, read and experienced in the last 35 years and publish in my daily motivational video messages on the Daily Locker Room website. I hope it will inspire and encourage you to improve your life, face challenges and set backs and guide you to work on yourself.

You may want to keep it in a visible place and pick it up often to read a message. There is an index in the front listing all messages and their page numbers which may help you to find a message that best fits the challenge ahead of you.

I dedicate this book, my body of work and my life to my beautiful and amazing daughter Nicole.

To all of you who I have shared my life with at my insurance company I'd like to thank each and every one of you for challenging and inspiring me to be my very best.

Thank you and I love you.

Eric J. Giglione

Index

"Happiness is not something ready made. It comes from our actions."

-Dalai Lama

Choose to be Happy

Every day we choose to be happy or not. Happiness is not a goal or a destination, it is a choice.

Twelve years ago, I was hit head-on while riding my motorcycle. I was hospitalized for many months and in rehab for years. I was encouraged by a number of patients who had serious issues like mine but still had wonderful attitudes. Other patients did not.

Although my situation looked bleak and I was in tremendous pain every day, I made the choice to remain in good spirits. How did I and others do it? Simple; I focused on the good things I had in my life, not what was bad or missing.

Twelve years later I still have that choice, and so do you. I can focus on what I can't do and don't have and be sad and depressed, or I can choose to focus on what I do have and can do! Let me challenge you today to do what I and so many others have done: decide to be happy!

Are You Coachable

Have you ever seen anyone who has achieved greatness without the help of other people? There is not one successful person on this planet who got there on his or her own. I remember John Maxwell saying: "There is no such thing as a self made – man or self-made millionaire and if there is, you haven't made much."

From the beginning of your journey in life, there were teachers, coaches, friends, and family members who came into your life to teach you, if you were coachable. Are you coachable?

I think one of the biggest challenges people face is themselves, their ego and pride. Remember, pride comes before the fall. The most successful, happy people I know are the most coachable people I've met.

Go and seek out others who can help in different areas of your life. In your personal life, friends, maybe counselors, can give you good personal advice and input on some of the challenges you are facing. Read some of the material that has been produced by people who have been in your situation and have come out on the other side. When you are coachable, you will trim off years of mistakes because you were wise enough to learn from others who already made them.

If you are a father, seek the advice of those fathers whom you respect and admire and follow their lead. I do this all the time. I reach out to my friends who are great fathers, great husbands, great in business and I listen, take notes and then I go do!

Encourage Someone to Dream

Have you ever worked toward a dream, but felt worn out by the uphill climb? At times like this, you need encouragement – someone to remind you about what it will be like when you get to the finish line. We all need each other more than we know.

You may be facing challenges that you can't overcome on your own; having a friend to walk with can get you through those times. In the same way, you have something to share with others to help them along their journey. You encourage others in their dreams and cheer them on as they go. When you believe in people, it gives their faith a boost. Your acts of kindness may be just what they needed to push on to victory.

Encourage someone today and as you do you will start to notice others encouraging you. Be grateful for the people that have been put in your life. Encourage them and they will encourage you. As you give, it will be given back to you!

Grow an Attitude of Gratitude

Everyone has an attitude. What's yours? Attitudes are contagious... the question is, is yours worth catching? The attitude to which I'm referring is an attitude of gratitude. Are you focused on all the things that are wrong in your life, or are you grateful for what you already have?

I believe this is a large part of why people get depressed. They're focused on what they don't have instead of what they do have.

So let's start today by making a list of those things for which we are grateful, such as our health, our arms, our legs, our eyes, our ears, our parents or siblings, our job, or living in America. Write down all these things and look at them.

If you do this every day and look at those things for which you are grateful, I promise you'll grow an attitude of gratitude, and everyone wants to be around people who are grateful.

Humility

Rick Pitino, the great basketball coach, says in his book, titled The One Day Contract: "The longer I live and the more I experience, the more I believe that humility is the quality essential to sustained success, and a lack of it is the major stumbling block for those who find success for a time, then lose it."

He continues: "Either you learn its value, or life drills it into you - and life can be a painful teacher. It is a lesson best learned before life makes you another case study."

Humility's twin brother is gratitude. When we are humble, we display gratitude in great abundance.

Pitino goes on to say: "That's why you see people like John Wooden, maybe the greatest coach of all time in any sport, or Mike Kryzyzewski, who is the modern-day John Wooden, sustain success for so long... You can readily see their humility. That doesn't mean they don't have flaws, don't get angry or make mistakes. Everybody does. But the key that opens up all the greatness is humility."

Keep Fighting

Sometimes life seems so unfair. You might have gone through a series of losses or setbacks, and it's easy to think it will never get better, maybe this is just my lot in life. If you are not careful, your negative thoughts will create a self-fulfilling prophecy.

I was entering the peak of my life, 45 years old, and had it all going on. Then one day I got hit on my Harley, and would find myself struggling to get my life back as I experienced some of the most challenging times of my life.

I learned then that you must keep fighting, you cannot give up. When you get knocked down it is a test of your inner courage and fortitude. If you are not careful, as you go through these challenges in life, it could make your mind spiral out of control.

It begins with one unfair situation, then we magnify it by having and holding on to the wrong mindsets. I'm asking you to break out of that rut! Remember, as Yogi Berra said, "It ain't over till it's over!" You may be down, but you're not out! Your best days are not behind you, they are in front of you.

When it looks like it just couldn't get any worse, that's the time that you need to stand up and fight. I know this personally because following the accident that almost claimed my life, some of the most exciting and positive things happened.

Keep standing and keep fighting. Your situation will begin to turn around when you least expect it!

Find Your Diamonds

Most of us are given the chance to reach the level of wealth, happiness, and success we want. Each of us passes by a lifetime of opportunity on a daily basis. What we need to keep in mind is that opportunity is also the master of camouflage. Opportunity doesn't carry a huge sign that says, "Opportunity." We have to be intelligent enough to examine every situation and ask ourselves, "What is this situation trying to teach me? What opportunity exists?"

Russell Herman Conwell, the founder of Temple University, traveled the country telling the classic story "Acres of Diamonds." An African farmer heard about huge fortunes from diamond mines. The farmer wanted to be rich, so he sold his farm and began to search the African continent for diamonds. He spent the rest of his life in fruitless pursuit of diamonds. Eventually broke, despondent, and desperate, he threw himself into a river and drowned.

The man who bought his farm discovered that the land was loaded with diamonds and ended up with one of the richest deposits in the world. If someone else's pasture looks greener, perhaps it is getting better care. Take action and discover acres of diamonds right in your own back yard!

Write Your Vision

Most businesses have a mission or vision statement that talks about the purpose and direction of the company. Every person should also have their own mission statement. What's your purpose? What are you dreaming about? What are your goals? How are you going to use your talents and abilities?

Many people have vague ideas about where they're headed in life, but something almost supernatural happens when you write down your vision and make a plan. It brings an inner resolve to the surface. No longer is that idea just a dream, now it's something you can look at every day. The people around you can see it too. You'll never know how others can help you achieve your goals. If they can see your vision they can run with it!

I want to encourage you not to live vaguely day to day. Don't be a wandering generality; instead become a meaningful specific. Make the decision to write down your dreams and vision.

If our leaders in government, business, and academics have a vision, so should you! Begin by writing it down.

"We must accept finite disappointment, but never lose infinite hope."

-Martin Luther King, Jr.

Laughter, the Best Medicine of All

If you want to live more, learn to laugh more. Start by laughing at yourself because you could easily do that. By not taking yourself and others too seriously, you'll achieve what experts call a "lighter heart." It will bring healing to your heart and mind. When was the last time you watched a funny movie? When was the last time you had a good belly laugh?

Remember as a kid when you laughed for no reason till it hurt? I see this with my daughter and her friends. We all did this, and then we grew up and stopped laughing.

Laughter has been proven to reduce stress and is medicine for your heart. People will want to be around you more, because your good sense of humor can make them laugh.

Let me encourage you today to laugh more often. Have more fun, go to an amusement park, or visit the circus when it's in town. Laugh more and it will not only add years to your life, it will add more quality to those years! Laughter is great medicine.

Release the Past

It's been said that the majority of conversations by men over 40 are about the past. Sometimes it's about the "good old days" and sometimes it's about dreams gone bad, "if I only had" stories, missed opportunities, etc. Letting our past 'sins and mistakes' dominate our thinking robs us of our present joy and our future happiness. It causes us to miss the real opportunity of today!

John Maxwell, in his outstanding best seller, Failing Forward, gives some great practical advice: "To move forward today, you must learn to say goodbye to yesterday's hurts, tragedies and baggage. You can't build a monument to past problems and fail forward."

Your best days are definitely ahead of you if you treat your mistakes as necessary lessons to be learned. Many people can't achieve success because they won't leave their pasts behind.

When I was growing up, I had no idea that my future would be in sales or sales management. I went to school for electronics and found myself very unhappy on the assembly line. Was this a mistake? No! I learned that while my whole family worked with their hands, I was dangerous with a screw driver so I'm glad I found this out. It was not a mistake, it was a lesson on don't always do what your family thinks you should – follow your heart and do what you were called to do.

One of the best teachings I ever heard on this came from Barbra Streisand. She said, "In life, there are no mistakes, only lessons to be learned."

Get Back Up Again

Life is full of things that try to push us down. We all face disappointments and setbacks. Maybe you received some bad news about your health, or perhaps a relationship didn't work out. That was a setback. It's easy to get discouraged or lose your enthusiasm or even be tempted to just settle where you are.

But if we're going to see our best lives come to pass, we have to have a bounce back mentality. That means when you get knocked down, you don't stay down. You get back up again. You have to know that every time adversity comes against you, it's a setup for a comeback!

There is no challenge too difficult, no obstacle too high, no sickness, no disappointment, no person... nothing that can keep you from your God-given destiny. If you stay in faith, then the universe, God, whatever you want to call it, will turn what was meant to be a stumbling block into a stepping stone, and you'll move forward in strength, ready for the victory.

Your Imagination is a Canvas

It all starts with your imagination, which is like a canvas. You can paint on it any kind of picture you choose through your thoughts, attitudes, and focus.

Don't let doubt or fear paint on your canvas. Don't let "impossible" or "can't be done" thoughts blur the colors on your canvas.

Instead, take out the paint brush of expectancy and hope and begin painting a bright future on the canvas of your mind and heart.

The kind of mental picture you paint is the goal toward which you will move. That image will set the direction for your life. If you want to change your life, you need to change the picture you're painting in your mind.

Programming your mind for success doesn't happen automatically. Each day, you must choose to expect good things to happen to you.

I want to encourage you to paint pictures of success, overcoming adversity, helping others and being relentless until the job is done. Then celebrate and go after something else, something bigger even more exciting, and start the next painting.

Born Creative with Imagination

Henry Ford said, "Anybody can do anything that he imagines." Creativity and imagination are frequently thought to be uncommon attributes of only a gifted few. That is not true. Creativity and imagination are a part of everyone's natural assets. They are as much a part of you as your heart, arms, and legs. You have a vast storehouse of both creativity and imagination.

It is up to you to discover and utilize them. Utilizing your creativity requires discipline, concentrated effort, and hard work. Creative people are awake and eager. They are always learning, producing, and thinking. Their endeavors give them pleasure and satisfaction.

Ralph Waldo Emerson said, "Imitation is suicide." If you are satisfied to just compete or imitate, you must be satisfied to be just average. You will earn the same rewards as everyone else. Here is a wonderful rule to follow; 'Create, don't compete.' If you create, the sky is the limit.

Take action today by working hard to stimulate your creativity and imagination. See everything as a creative challenge. Look for new alternatives and new combinations for simple and ordinary things. Ask, "Can I make it a little bit better?"

Start Thinking and Dreaming Bigger

I want to flat-out encourage you today to dream bigger dreams. If you are going to think, you might as well think big! Many people settle for too little and they allow complacency to keep them in mediocrity. They get comfortable where they are and are afraid to step up because of pre-programming, their past and where they come from.

"My parents were poor... Nobody in my family has ever amounted to much, so guess I won't either... I've gone as far as I can with my education." We've all heard these excuses. You can go further than your parents ever went. I say that with no disrespect to your parents, but you and I should do better than our parents did, and our children should do better than we do.

Maybe you were raised in a negative environment, where everybody around you was critical, down in the dumps, and discouraging. You may be tempted to use your upbringing as an excuse to live the same way. Don't pass that junk down to your children; stop that negative cycle. You can be the one to break the curse in your family.

You can affect future generations by the decisions you make today. Make the best decision ever by daring to dream bigger dreams.

"In life, there are not mistakes, only lessons to be learned."

-Barbara Streisand

Have Fun and Enjoy Every Day

You might be saying to me, "I would have fun if I had your life." The reason I am living the life I am living is because I always found a way to have fun no matter what I was doing. How many of you have met people who go to work miserable, complaining, and negative about work, so they think that the only time they can have fun is when they are not working.

Think about it. If you can find a way to have fun when you go to work, school, or parent your children, then you will bring that most important energy to your day.

It is simple. Fall in love with your work first! The way to love your work is to be very good at it. Improve daily whatever it is that your doing wether at work, home, school or with your friends and you too can have a little bit of fun every day.

Do You Cloud Up or Rain?

Years ago, I went to a seminar and the speaker said something that I never forgot. He was talking about how there are people who like to talk about what they are going to do and then there are people who just do it. As he was explaining it he said: "some people just cloud up well, but don't rain." What was he saying? He was saying that some people can talk a good game, know exactly what to say, sound really good and even look the part. But when you get behind the curtain, you see that while some people talk a good game, they cloud up well, but they just don't rain.

I want us to be rainmakers. People who make it rain mean what they say and say with they mean, they make it a point to talk less and do more, they under promise over deliver. If they tell you they are going to do something, they do it! No excuses. They make commitments and if they can't keep them, they communicate to the person to whom they have committed and work it out.

When you become this kind of a person, others will open the doors wide for you. Opportunities that slip past others will not get past you. People will go out of their way to support and help you in whatever areas you need support because you are a rainmaker.

Attitude is Everything

Tap into the power of your attitude to transform it into action. Attitude is everything; it impacts everything you do. The American Heritage Dictionary defines attitude as 'a state of mind or feeling with regard to some matter'. Attitude for me can be defined in one word: life!

Your attitude makes an incredible difference in your life. It can be a powerful tool for positive action.
A bad attitude can be a poison that cripples your ability to fulfill your potential. Your attitude dictates whether you are living life or life is living you. Attitude determines whether you are on the way or in the way. See your challenges as opportunities to learn and see the good in every bad situation.

Grow an attitude that believes you will reach your goals. The next time you are faced with a difficult challenge, focus on staying positive. Your setbacks can be setups for even greater opportunities. Like our cars, give yourself a little tune up, a checkup from the neck up. Climb higher with a more positive attitude and live your very best life!

Become Solution Minded

There are two kinds of people in the world: those who are part of the problem, and those who are part of the solution. Which are you? Each of us makes our own choice to be a problem-minded person or a solution-minded person. It is not what happens to you that matters as much as how you react or respond to each circumstance and situation. Your reaction determines your success, not what happens.

If your partner breaks up with you, you can respond by getting upset and angry, or you could respond by asking what happened. Why did this relationship not work and what can I learn from this? Most of us blame the other person and while there is often truth in that, the only way we can grow is to focus on the things we can control, what we did and what we could have done differently.

The happiest people are not people without problems. They are people who have learned how to solve their problems. You can alter the pattern of your life dramatically by altering even just slightly the pattern of your thinking. You change from a problem person who thinks like a victim to a solution person by changing from a negative thinker to positive thinker.

When things look bleak, you become sad, depressed, upset, uncertain, or negative. But remember, you can change your thinking. We are probably the only creatures on earth with that powerful ability. Dwelling on the negative only has a negative influence on our lives. Conversely, the more positively you think, talk and act, the brighter, happier and more successful your life will become.

Be Prepared

If you want to get on the wrong side your coworkers, make a habit of showing up late and unprepared for meetings. Most people believe they're already wasting precious minutes by being stuck in a meeting, and if you wander in last with nothing to add you can be sure you'll be getting the stink eye.

On the other hand, if you take all of your meetings seriously and show up to each on time and with ideas that you researched in advance, not only will you impress your coworkers, you'll also win points with your boss or clients.

Though your boss and colleagues might not want to use the ideas you present, you'll at least prove to them that you're a confident, creative thinker, that you're dedicated to your work, and that you're a team player.

These are the kinds of strong qualities leaders look for when they're considering who to promote and who deserves to get ahead.

Fight Back and Never Look Back

Someone once said, "You are either an optimist or a pessimist; a realist is a pessimist in disguise." Optimists fight back when they hit a setback. They are resilient in the face of the rejections and disappointments we all face at one time or another in our lives. Optimists pick themselves up quickly and go on. They bounce back.

Pessimists, on the other hand, succumb. They give up. They get depressed. They throw in the towel and let life run them over. The only thing that separates optimists from pessimists is the way they think. When optimists have setbacks, they assume the problem or its consequences won't last very long and they don't indulge in self-blame. Instead they look to see if there's anything they could do to prevent the same things from happening in the future and they don't jump to the conclusion that this setback will ruin everything.

You can become more optimistic by practicing this alternative thinking about setbacks, and every inch you move toward optimism means another inch of resiliency. It means you'll bounce back sooner from the inevitable setbacks of life. It means you'll have greater personal strength and persistence and more of your life will go the way you want it to go.

Negativity is a Habit – So is Positivity

By now, you know it's important to think positively and think of the future in an uplifting way. But that's not always so easy. Do you melt down in times of crisis? Do you sometimes let a negative inner voice get the best of you? Do you allow those nasty little thoughts to take control of your day, week, month, and even life? Work on breaking that cycle.

First, take some quiet time by yourself to identify where that voice is coming from. Whose voice is it: the voice of someone from your childhood, a teacher, a parent, some childhood friend? Most likely, that voice isn't your own, and recognizing whose it is will be the first step to stopping it.

When I realized that my loving dad's voice was in my head when he told me one day that I would never amount to anything, my world changed for many years and I never thought I would become anyone and would be doomed to a life of failure.

Once I identified the voice, I took action and quieted that voice by realizing that he did not know what he was saying or doing and it was easy to tell that voice in my head (not my father) to shut up! Tell yourself that you are awesome, lovable, successful, and filled with all kinds of talent and abilities. Kick the negativity habit and live your best life!

Enjoy the Journey

Sometimes it's easy to become so goal-oriented and so focused on our dreams that we overlook the simple things we should be enjoying in our everyday life. We have to remember that life is not really about the destination, it's about how we live along the way. It's about the path we're on that shines brighter and brighter.

In this life, there is no such thing as a finish line. Once you accomplish one dream, there will be another for you to go after. When you overcome one challenge, there will be another. There is always another mountain to climb. If we make the mistake of just living for the destination, we'll look up one day and realize we've missed out on the biggest part of life, because most of life is routine. Most of us get up every morning, go to work, come home, eat dinner, go to bed and do it again.

There are very few mountaintops, like when you graduate from school, or you get married, or have a child, or go on vacation. The high times can be few and far between. Don't get stuck living only for the mountaintops. Learn to enjoy the path you're on now. Learn to enjoy the people in your life. Learn to enjoy the simple blessings every day. True success can be found in our daily lives. I remember years ago listening to Earl Nightingale who said: "It's the person you become in pursuit of those goals that really matters in life."

"Life is a journey, not a destination."

-Ralph Waldo Emerson

Failure is Not What You Think

If you knew you wouldn't fail, what activity would you try? If you knew that success would be guaranteed in furthering your education, a relationship, your career, or any endeavor, what would you do?

We don't have problems achieving goals. The problem is that we don't set them to begin with because we are afraid of failure. Fear of failure, fear of success, fear of the unknown, fear paralyzes us, you and me, from taking the leap of faith.

Fear of failure is what prevents people from giving their very best. Their attitude is, "Why try? I'm probably not going to make it, so why try that hard and get disappointed? I'll try it but if things get to tough, no big deal."

Nothing worthwhile has ever been accomplished without someone saying, "I refuse to give up!" This attitude comes from the belief that there's no such thing as failure except in no longer trying.

Give your best effort at everything you do. Something good will come out of it even if it doesn't turn out the way you want. Keep the right perspective and see the good in everything. You have everything to gain and nothing lose! "You miss 100% of the shots you don't take," said Wayne Gretsky, the famous hockey player. Failure is only failure when you stop trying, so keep trying and enjoy the ride!

Find Your Inspiration

An inspired person changes the world. Why? Because they have the passion and conviction necessary to move their environment. How do you find your inspiration? For me, I found it first in my music. I played an instrument and loved it! So as a youth I was inspired. So were you if you played baseball or did ballet or acted in the school play.

Inspiration is found when we lose ourselves in our work and in our play. I played tennis for years and was inspired to play great and I did. I fell in love with my work and because of it my work fell in love with me and rewarded me beyond my wildest imagination.

So where do you start? Exactly where you are right now. Whatever you are about to do after reading this message, get inspired to do it and see it as an opportunity to make a difference. If you are going to coach your son's elementary school soccer team, give those kids your heart and soul, and be inspired.

If you are about to go to work, give your work the passion and inspiration it needs so that you can live an inspired, great life. If you are about to spend time with your significant other, really be inspired and excited to be with this person.

Refocus on the Mission

Ralph Waldo Emerson observed, "Concentration is the secret of strength in politics, in war, in trade, in short, in all management of human affairs." Where should you focus that concentration? On the mission.

And when you make a mistake, don't chase after it. Don't try to defend it. Don't throw good money after it. Just refocus your attention on the mission and then move on. You must always keep your eye on what it is you desire to do. I have yet to meet a person focused on yesterday who had a better tomorrow.

John Foster Dulles, secretary of state in the Eisenhower administration, observed, "The measure of success is not whether you have a tough problem to deal with, but whether it is the same problem you had last year." A problem solved is a springboard to future success, to bigger and better things. The key is to focus on what you are learning, not on what you are losing. If you do that, then you will open the door to future possibilities.

A positive attitude can help you do that. It can help you learn from the present and look into the future. Norman Vincent Peale said, "Positive thinking is how you think about a problem. Enthusiasm is how you feel about a problem. The two together determine what you do about a problem." And that's what really matters in the end.

"If you have a tough problem that won't go away, check to make sure your attitude isn't at fault." – John C. Maxwell in The Difference Maker.

Take a Risk

In life, there are no safe places or risk-free activities. Helen Keller, author, speaker, and advocate for disabled persons, asserted, "Security is mostly a superstition. It does not exist in nature, nor do the children of men as a whole experience it. Avoiding danger is no safer in the long run than outright exposure. Life is either a daring adventure or nothing."

Everything in life brings risk. It's true that you risk failure if you try something bold because you might miss it. But you also risk failure if you stand still and don't try anything new. G.K. Chesterton wrote, "I do not believe in a fate that falls on men however they act; but I do believe in a fate that falls on them unless they act."

The less you venture out, the greater your risk of failure. Ironically, the more you risk failure – and actually fail – the greater your chances of success.

This was a very hard concept for me at first, as it may be for you. I highly recommend that you move forward and don't worry about the outcome, positive or negative, because it is neither. When you take a risk you are saying to the world, "Regardless of what happens, I'm excited, I'm going after it with everything I've got in me!"

Mistakes Happen – No Whining

We all make mistakes. It's part of being human. It's perfectly okay to make mistakes. But once the mistakes are made, learn from them and then forget them. Don't continue to carry them as excess baggage.

Remember, just about all our concerns resolve themselves one way or another so you can stop worrying. The sooner you do, the happier you will be. You can devote yourself to things that are significant, and over which you can determine the solutions and outcomes replacing worry with action!

The tragedy of many people's lives is that worry robs them of the sense that they are competent to cope with life's challenges. They are so consumed by worry that they don't trust their own minds, instincts and abilities. They don't feel capable of asserting their own legitimate interests and needs. When the going gets tough, they crumble.

Let me encourage you today to stop worrying! It is robbing you of a great life waiting to be lived. Worrying will not solve a single problem or challenge. Live your very best life by replacing worry with positive action!

Enthusiasm – it's Greek

Ralph Waldo Emerson said, "Nothing great was ever achieved without enthusiasm." The word enthusiasm comes from the Greek word entheos, which means 'the god within'. Enthusiasm is one of your greatest assets. It is more important than money, power or influence. Enthusiasm is energy, direction, purpose, and commitment.

With properly directed enthusiasm, you can acquire anything you want. Happy, successful people have learned to think and act enthusiastically. Enthusiastic people are in control of their lives. People who create and maintain 'the god within' make a difference in their lives and the lives of others.

All great achievements have enthusiasm as the foundation. Look at any successful organization or person and you will find them consumed with a specific goal, absolutely confident in their abilities, and faithful in the purpose of their endeavors. They are committed to something in which they find enjoyment, challenge, and deep satisfaction in achievement.

So take action today and join the most successful people in the world. Live each day enthusiastically and you will have greater vitality and zest. Your enthusiasm will be contagious to others. Become more enthusiastic! You will live your very best life and take a bunch of people with you!

"Positive thinking is how you think about a problem. Enthusiasm is how you feel about a problem. The two together determine what you do about a problem"

-Norman Vincent Peale

First Class Only

What is class? Though difficult to truly define, elements of class include humility, poise, confidence, and healthy pride. Other components are compassion, understanding, self-responsibility, and consideration of the effects of one's actions.

Class never runs scared. It is the knowledge that you can meet life head-on and handle whatever comes along. If you have class, you have one of the intangible assets that few possess. People of class are those who make you want to climb higher. They give you hope that there are some good people out there.

People of class do not necessarily have the most expensive clothes, cars, homes, or material things. Often, the classiest people don't have most of the material trappings. You cannot buy class; you must earn it through your actions and how you carry yourself.

Make a decision today to live a first-class life, and in so doing you will give the world greater hope.

Discover Your Calling

It's not as hard as you think to discover your calling. Take notice of what you love to do. If it's the love of the technical aspects of how things work, lean toward engineering, computers, and other sciences. If it's the love of working with people, then it's communications, public relations, sales, leadership. Maybe it's a field that combines both areas.

The next step is to narrow down your "list" to the thing(s) you're good at and love doing. Learn more and get better each day. This will reveal specifically which road to follow. One man loved golf and was very good at it, but couldn't make it as a pro. He kept learning about the game. One thing led to another and he started writing articles about golf. Not long after, the magazine Golf Digest found its way into the world!

The amazing thing is that if you find something you're good at and love, the lines between work and play will blur and you might have discovered your calling. Work hard and positive feedback will follow. If you're wondering about money, just know that if you find your calling, money will find you!

1% Inspiration, 99% Perspiration

Life is what we decide it is. We are in charge, we have control. For most people, that thought is a problem. They never decide what they want. People do not have much trouble achieving goals. The problem is they do not set goals in the first place.

People do not plan to fail. They just fail to plan. They leave their success to chance, but chance does not work. Thomas Edison said, "Genius is 1% inspiration and 99% perspiration." Most geniuses have ordinary intelligence and become geniuses because they use their mind to work harder than others.

What are the qualities that geniuses possess? They have a creative, open mind that is receptive to new ideas and different ways of solving problems. They approach problems systematically, using orderly processes to reach well-thought-out conclusions. They take action and concentrate intensely and single-mindedly on the task at hand. They set goals!

Nothing great was ever attained without concentrated effort and energy focused on a single objective. Successful people adopt a specific purpose that becomes all consuming. They use 1% inspiration and 99% perspiration to live their best life. You can too!

Look for the Good

It's been said that we should see the good in every person and situation. While most of us agree that this makes sense, we don't always think and act this way. Seeing the good in every bad situation, or seeing 'the glass half full instead of half empty', will give you the advantage of the right emotions and attitude necessary to win in life.

Sales professionals understand that when you see the good in people, regardless of their initial attitude, they usually end up becoming your best customers. If you look for the good in your career, friends, mates, or people you meet, then the good in those people or situations have a chance to come out.

First, be grateful and take inventory of the many things that you've taken for granted: a healthy body, a loving family, financial success, etc. Next, stay focused on your dreams and goals at all times. Finally, know that everything that you want out of life you'll get through people. So make it a habit to see the good in every person you meet and express that feeling to them.

Challenges are Blessings

If you're like me, you sometimes find yourself in some tough spots, and not sure what to do. I have heard it said that, "Challenges and setbacks come into your life to help you grow." First things first, life is neither easy nor fair, so let's get that out of the way. Don't look for an easy road because the road to success is always under construction.

In my business, we grow leaders. We know that leaders do not develop in a day, they develop and grow over time. We teach them first to take full responsibility for every result, both good and bad. It's easy to take responsibility when you hit a home run or get an A on your report card, but not so easy when you strike out or get an F. Many people blame someone or something else to avoid taking responsibility and doing something about it.

So if you want to overcome whatever challenges you are facing right now, take responsibility for the results. Decide that you are going to be proactive. Take positive steps to overcome, fix, or simply plow through that challenge or obstacle.

I Don't Have the Time

When someone fails do something and says, "I didn't have the time," it is not true. What they are really saying is, "I didn't do it because it just wasn't high on my priority list." We all have time to do the things we really want to do. Better life management is simply a matter of priorities.

We use an amazingly small amount of time earning a living, improving our skills, increasing our knowledge, and preparing for the future. The important thing about time is not to waste it with activities that do not promote personal growth or do not bring enjoyment. Never find yourself with time on your hands.

Take action today! When you want to relax and enjoy some leisure activity, do it with no guilt because you planned it. When you are working, be passionate and spend your time being positive and productive! When you are with your children, really be with them! You have all the time you need to accomplish what you want out of life. All you need to do is respect time and it will respect you back.

Associate with Winners

Most people underestimate the power of negativity and negative words. The way to insure success and happiness is to associate with winners. These are people with a positive attitude, who are trying their best, and enjoying life. There will always be people out there who will be negative no matter what. If you are not careful, they will affect your attitude.

Since sending out 'The Daily Locker Room', there have been so many people who have reached out to say, "thank you." These folks mention that they enjoy reading it every day (mission accomplished!). These people want to be motivated, have dreams, and see the good in people and life. Then there are those who have been very negative, and some have even threatened me. Can you believe it?

I can, and here's why. There are a lot of people out there who are hurting and sometimes they will try to hurt other people. If I listened to these people, I would have stopped sending the 'Locker Room'. That will not happen!

Let me encourage you not to give negative people a second thought. Associate with winners; people who will encourage and lift you up.

Choose Success for Your Future

Your words have creative power. With your words, you can either bless or curse your future. If you want to know what your life is going to be like five years from now, just listen to what you're saying about yourself today.

Too many people go around saying, "I'll never get well. I'll never get out of debt," or, "It's flu season. I'll probably get it," or, "This marriage is never going to last." Then they wonder why they don't see things turn around. It's because they're calling defeat into their future. They're calling in mediocrity. Don't let that be you!

When you wake up in the morning, no matter how you feel or what things look like, instead of using your words to describe your situation, use your words to change your situation. Make a declaration of faith by saying, "This is going to be a great day. I succeed at whatever I set my hands to do." When you do that, you are choosing to bless your future. You are calling in favor, increase and opportunities. You are opening the door for the universe to move on your behalf so you can live the abundant life that is in store for you!

Success is a choice, but so is failure. Stop calling in failure and start calling in success.

"Anybody can do anything that he imagines."

-Henry Ford

Live Passionately

One day Tom Sawyer's aunt gave him the chore of painting the fence. While at first Tom was not excited about this, he decided to get passionate about it anyway. His friends saw him singing and having a great time and got very jealous. They asked if they could help paint the fence, so Tom handed out brushes. What would have been a long, boring project took half the time, and Tom and his friends had a ball doing it!

So what are you waiting for? If you get passionate doing even the small things, your life will take on new meaning and purpose. Your passion will be contagious. If you get passionate about your dreams and goals, people will get excited being around you! Whatever you get excited about will return the same excited energy back to you!

So take action today and do everything with greater passion. Whether you work full time, go to school, or are raising a family, no matter what you do, decide to do it with greater passion. You will make your world and the world around you a much more exciting place.

The Driving Force

Goals are the driving force behind every great invention, achievement and breakthrough. You must have goals if you plan on living an exciting, worthwhile life. If this is true, and it is, why do so few people have clearly defined goals?

I believe the main reason is because they have not gotten serious enough about what they would like to accomplish. Instead of setting goals for today, tomorrow, this week, next year, and 10 years from now, they settle for whatever comes their way.

Let me encourage you today to take action. Write down 10 things that you would like to accomplish, achieve or obtain. Take a look at that list and then rank them in order of importance. Develop 2 or 3 action steps toward achieving each goal. Finally, set a timetable for when you would like to achieve them.

My friends, if you do this—and I pray you will—it will put you in the Top 5% of the most successful people on this planet! Look at your goals often, and let them be the driving force behind every choice and action.

It's a New Day

There will never be another day like this one. It's unique, one of a kind. In it are the joys, adventures, challenges and opportunities that can only be found in a single day. Are you going to appreciate and make the most of this day or will you treat it like just another day? Each day is a present, a gift like no other. Dragging in the pain of yesterday or the fear of tomorrow will rob you of an exciting and fulfilling day today!

When people are asked; "how are you doing today?" a common response is, "same ol' same ol'" or "same BS different day." So how do you avoid this negativity and guarantee that each day will be cherished? The first step is to be grateful that you have been given this day. Grow an attitude of gratitude! This single thought of gratitude will make today like no other.

Make a decision to live this day to the fullest by living in the moment! Don't think about yesterday or worry about tomorrow. Take action and treat each day as if it were your last and see your spirits rise higher. Do this and you will live a life of greater joy and happiness by living one day at a time!

It's All in How You Frame it

Feeling happy is not as easy as just saying. "I'm happy!" or, "Things are great!" But that sort of attitude doesn't hurt. You can trick your brain into believing things are going well or poorly in your life.

It's all in how you frame it. The happiest people out there aren't always the ones who had great childhoods, were successful early in life, or were born beautiful. They're the people who, when they create the story of their lives, create a story in which they're the hero, not the victim.

If you can work to see the glass as half full, see the silver lining in a cloudy day, and find a way to paint your memoirs in a positive light, you're on your way to a life filled with happiness. Here are some of the mantras (affirmations) that you can begin your day with to get yourself on the right path:

"I am love, I am loved."
"I will enjoy myself today."
"No matter what happens, I won't judge myself."
"Today will be a good day!"

See the glass half full, see the good in every perceived bad situation. Look for the good in others and you will find it. See the good in life and you will attract more good.

The Law of Connection

It's been said that, "people don't care how much you know until they know how much you care." The leadership trainer John Maxwell describes The Law of Connection this way: "you must first touch a heart, before you ask for a hand." In life, everything you want to have, achieve and do will happen through people. The most influential and successful people in the world share one trait; they know how to connect with people.

So how can you better connect with people? Start by listening, really listening. Take time to understand what they are saying and why. Steven Covey said, "seek first to understand, then to be understood." The more time you take to understand your friends, family, peers, boss, or any one you meet, the more connected you will become with them.

Take action today! The next time you're with someone, listen–really listen–then observe how they listen to your concerns, thoughts and ideas. Together we can make this world a better place, one person at time, one day at a time, by listening to one another. Let's all get connected!

Be Willing to Make Sacrifices

Since the beginning of time man has been making sacrifices in order to make progress in the areas of education, science, medicine, sports, business and family. There can be no great accomplishments without sacrifice. If you want to achieve anything great, you must count the cost and willingly pay the price for success. The greater our sacrifices are, the greater the rewards are; no pain, no gain.

Instinctively we know this is true, yet so many people are unwilling to make sacrifices in order to achieve success? Why? Some think it's because people are lazy. But according to some experts, the real reason is to avoid pain. Yet without pain, nothing great happens. Your mother went through extreme amounts of pain in order to bring you into the world. It started there and has never stopped.

Make a quality decision today to enter the world of the most successful people and decide exactly what it is that you want to accomplish, then be willing to make necessary sacrifices knowing that those sacrifices will produce the dreams and goals you desire!

"You must first reach a heart, before you ask for a hand."

-John Maxwell

Use Feedback to Your Advantage

People will sometimes give me their opinion or feedback on a variety of issues. Unfortunately, more often than I care to admit, my immediate reaction is to defend myself or what I am doing. Upon reflection I have found that this always limits my opportunity to grow.

Over the years I have learned to use feedback to my advantage and grow from it. This often has made the difference between success and failure. I am only one person with my own thoughts. When I allow others to give me their opinions and feedback, I have more resources from which to make a decision.

In fact, my greatest life lessons have come from my biggest critics. Winston Churchill, during the most difficult time in his nation's history, gathered his harshest critics and solicited their opinions. He utilized much of their thinking in order to bring England out of its darkest days.

Don't waste another minute! Use all the feedback you receive to climb higher and achieve a life of excellence.

Are You on the Computer?

The other day I walked into this men's clothing store in downtown NYC. This store caught my attention because the window was amazing! The style was cool, so I walked in the store and like some of you most seasoned and veteran shoppers out there, I started scanning the store and was excited about what I was seeing.

Well, this went on for about five minutes and no one had greeted me, nor come over to me. I headed to the front door, looked to my right at the sales person, and saw he was on his computer. He looked up, almost like I was interrupting him, and waved goodbye to me.

I thought to myself after I walked out, 'thank God he did not greet me because my wallet would be in pain right now!'

How many of you are on the computer when you should be paying attention to your business or your career! I see it all the time, people who are not giving their best in their work then struggle and complain about everything.

I want to encourage all of you today to get off the cell phone, get off the computer and go do whatever you do with complete focus, passion and relentless pursuit.

Fake It Till You Make It

People with the best attitude naturally rise to the top. They expect good things to happen to them. Usually they get what they expect - not through magic, but because they become the kind of people worthy of their good fortune. First, you must become the person you want to be in your mind. My mother used to say to me, "Fake it till you make it."

To develop a good attitude, begin conducting yourself as though you already have a good attitude. Successful people have good attitudes. They are convinced that they can accomplish what they set out to accomplish. For them, achievement is natural and there is no good reason why they cannot achieve all that they want. They bounce back quickly from defeat and see it as a lesson on the road to success.

Successful people expect more good than bad out of life. They expect to succeed more often than they fail, and they do! Unexpected sources of help come to people who are positive, enthusiastic and cheerful. Make a decision to join those who have developed a successful attitude. See yourself living your very best life; you deserve no less!

Never Give Up

When asked about the key to his success, British Prime Minister Winston Churchill summed it up in seven words: "Never give up. Never, never give up." The history of man is the story of turning defeat into victory, failure into success. If what we are doing is right for us and we have made up our minds to reach our goals, we have only to stay with it, minute by minute, hour by hour, day by day, until we succeed.

A little more persistence, a little more effort, a little more creative thinking can turn what seems like failure into glorious success. There is no failure except in quitting. There is no defeat except from within, no really insurmountable barrier except our own inherent weakness of purpose.

Successful people rarely get discouraged. They seldom walk around with their heads down. They have moments of doubt, concern and frustration, but they come roaring back. Problems and adversities make them dig their heels in and work harder if necessary. Quitting is not an option.

Successful people are dreamers who insist that their dreams, aspirations, and ideas are too important to remain fantasies. Their patience, perseverance, and never-give-up spirit are rewarded. Take action today and never, never give up!

We Become What We Think About

Earl Nightingale, after 30 years of research, determined the "secret" of success: "We become what we think about." Success is a matter of expectation. It is amazing how our thoughts, feelings and attitudes at the beginning of a project, game or idea influence the outcome.

If we expect to do well on a test, we do. If we expect to play tennis well, we do. No one wins all the time, but people who expect to win, win more often than people who expect to lose. Positive-thinking people seem to get that intangible edge that we often call "the breaks."

They expect to succeed just as they expect the sun to rise in the east. They create an habitual attitude and expectation of success. We must understand that first we must become that which we seek. Whatever we are looking for must first be found within us, whether it be success, happiness or peace of mind.

Take action today, and your world will soon change to reflect the new, emerging you. Before you can achieve the kind of life you want, you must first become the kind of person you expect others to be. If you want others to like you, you must be likable. It's called The Law of Cause and Effect and works 100% of the time!

Carpe Diem

People create success by focusing on today. Today is the only time you have. It's too late for yesterday and you can't depend on tomorrow. Most of the time we miss that. Why? Because we exaggerate yesterday. Our past successes and failures often look bigger to us in hindsight. Yesterday ended last night. Don't dwell on yesterday's success or failure. Learn from it and move forward.

We also overestimate tomorrow. William Allen White observed, "Multitudes of people have failed to live for today. They have spent their lives reaching for the future. What they have had within their grasp today they have missed entirely, because only the future has intrigued them . . . and the first thing they knew, the future became the past." Hoping for a good future without investing in today is like a farmer waiting for a crop without ever planting a seed.

Finally, we underestimate today. Have you ever asked someone what they were doing and they said, "Oh I'm just killing time." They might as well have said, "I'm just throwing away my life", or "I'm killing myself." Ben Franklin asserted that time is, "the stuff life is made of."

Today is the only time we have within our grasp. Cherish today and you'll live your very best life!

A Masterpiece

"The quality of your life will be determined by the level of commitment to excellence, no matter what your chosen field," said Vince Lombardi. Achieving excellence means making a commitment to excellence. It means making a decision that you are going to be the best at what you do. As long as you demand excellence and accept nothing less, you will assure yourself of success. The universal respect of excellence never changes.

Excellence is revered and commands the highest price. People who perform with excellence achieve internal comfort, joy, and satisfaction. Their work becomes a major source of accomplishment. They derive deep satisfaction from being 'uncommon people', producing excellent products or services.

These 'uncommon people' achieve a lifetime of internal security. They realize that there is always a market for the 'best', and never have to worry about their incomes. Great people such as Antonio Stradivarius, William Shakespeare, Leonardo da Vinci, and Thomas Chippendale created masterpieces. They performed with excellence not because of any external pressure, but because of their own internal insistence.

So decide today to be excellent at whatever you do and thrive to join the great masters.

Dig In

One thing I've learned is that whenever life seems extra difficult and the intensity has been turned up, it's a sure sign that you're close to victory. Whenever negative thoughts bombard your mind, or you're tempted to get discouraged, that's not the time to give up! That's the time to dig your heels in. That's the time to press on with a new attitude because you are closer than you think to your victory!

Perhaps you've had a lot go against you lately. It seems like the more you try, the worse things get. Maybe you are doing the right thing, but the wrong thing keeps happening. Instead of getting discouraged, say, "I've come too far to stop now, I've been through too much to back down, and I realize the reason the intensity has been turned up is because I'm about to give birth to my dreams!"

Don't allow your disappointments to steal your future! Instead, press on toward your goals. You've come too far to give up now; keep pressing forward toward those hopes and dreams and in the end, you'll be glad you did!

"A gossip is one who talks to you about others ... a bore is one who talks to you about himself ... and a brilliant conversationalist is one who talks to you about yourself."

-Lisa Kirk

Old Dog New Tricks?

We've all heard, "you can't teach an old dog new tricks." First things first: people are not dogs, and life is not a bag of tricks. The point of that saying is that people can't change. This is categorically untrue! History is filled with people who have moved in a whole new direction. It's a matter of internal motivation, drive and the determination to win.

How can you avoid the trap of thinking you can't change? If what are you doing is not working, move in a new direction and learn a new trick. At first it will be uncomfortable, but like all changes, it will become the new normal as you move forward.

So if you want different results than the ones you are getting, take action today and move in a new direction. Remember that insanity is doing the same thing over and over but expecting a different result. Do something new, learn something new, and see yourself climb higher.

Winning an Argument

Many people get trapped in debates they cannot win, not sure of what they're going to say, not anticipating what their adversary will say, failing to define their terms, and not even sure what the argument is all about. Can you avoid these snares? Pick your fights. Confront others only when you can predict at least a draw. Develop a reputation as someone who admits to being wrong when your errors are revealed to you. This encourages others to believe you when you assert yourself.

Know your adversary. Prepare for likely tactics and plan to push suspected hot buttons to get your way. Know why you're arguing. Do you have a need to win, to work off your aggressions, or to establish a pecking order in the barnyard? Do your reasons make sense? Provide an alternative for anything you may be arguing against. Don't knock down the ideas of others without having something to put in their place.

Let the other person speak first. Your adversary will become a better listener, and you will gain clues to what it will take to convince him or her. Keep your cool while revealing a well-modulated sense of annoyance, even anger. Save sarcasm for your toughest and most uncooperative adversaries.

Develop a win-win mentality in order to meet both your needs and those of the other person, rather than defending a one-sided and self-serving position. Never try to win by destroying an opponent. Attack issues, not people, and you will be living your very best life.

Success – What Is It?

Henry David Thoreau said, "If one advances confidently in the direction of his or her dreams and endeavors to live the life which he has imagined, he will meet with success unexpected in common hours". Note carefully the phrase 'in the direction of his dreams': not his parents', spouse's, or his friends' dreams, but his own dreams.

Live the life which you have imagined. If you are not doing what is right and comfortable for you, how can you expect to 'be right' for your parents, spouse, kids, friends, or your colleagues? Trying to fit into a mold created by someone else will likely lead to frustration, anxiety, and failure.

Success does not equate to wealth or status. It has nothing to do with what other people think about you. Success has only to do with your opinions of yourself and your actions. If you get to the point where you can enjoy every day, and cultivate your own sense of purpose, accomplishment and fulfillment; what more can you ask of life?

The best definition of success I've ever found is as follows, "Success is the progressive realization of a worthy goal."

It's Pouring Rain

Be pleasant and courteous to everyone you meet. Smile and give them a warm hello. It is just as easy to be warm and kind to people as it is be curt and mean. The results are amazing because your positive behavior makes you feel even better than the small joys you bring to others.

Try it for just one day. Treat everyone you come into contact with as the most important person on earth. Kindness to others is a catalyst for all kinds of positive effects in your life.

The other day, it was pouring rain. As I approached the door to a doughnut shop, a man was holding the door for me and getting soaked while doing it. I did not know this man at all. Wow! His small act of kindness gave me the motivation to be extra kind to others that day. It is amazing how we can be affected by other people's kindness. Why not be that person?

Kindness comes back to us in when we show it to others. Take action today, and be kind! You'll achieve calmness, tranquility and a deep inner peace.

Stop Procrastinating

Although putting off an unpleasant task from time to time is not serious, chronic stalling is a problem. You waste time worrying about what you have to do and your mind magnifies beyond all reality the pain you will experience by doing it and the risk of letting down the people who were counting on you to get things done on time.

Spend the next week invoking a 24-hour rule; respond to each new stimulus, be it email request, phone calls and so on within 24 hours.

When a new task looks overwhelming, start it immediately, even if you can only spend a few minutes on it.

Break every difficult task into manageable pieces and work on one piece each day. Stop thinking about how uncomfortable you think you'll feel while performing an undesirable task and start thinking about how good you'll feel when the job is done.

Write a schedule for completing your work and keep it in a highly visible place. And finally, reward yourself for making progress on a challenging project. Give yourself a bonus by doing something you really like!

Tell or Show

In the early years of my life I really believed people when they told me they were going to do something.

Whether it was agreeing to an appointment I set up for business, a date with a girl, or a night out with a friend, my attitude was if I tell you I am going to be somewhere or do something, you can take it to the bank.

As I grew up in life, I began to see that many people don't feel that way. They will tell you they are going to do something and in some cases, while they are telling you this, they have no intention of doing it. Some just want to look good in front of their boss.

What I've learned is that it doesn't matter what people say, it matters what they do. We don't promote people because they sound good, we promote them because they deliver the goods.

I remember years ago listening to Dr. Wayne Dyer and he said something that I will never forget: "what you are speaks so loudly I can't hear what you're saying."

"Fake it till you make it."

-Josephine Giglione

Your Best is Good Enough

All you can do is your best. If you commit to giving your best, you can assure yourself of ultimate success. As William James said, "If you will do each day as best you can the work which is before you, you will wake up one day and find yourself one of the competent ones of your generation."

Vince Lombardi said this about giving your best: "The dictionary is the only place that success comes before work. Hard work is the price we must all pay for success. I think we can accomplish almost anything if we are willing to pay the price and give our best effort. The price of success is hard work, dedication to the job at hand, and the determination that whether we win or lose, we have applied the best of ourselves to the task at hand."

Whether you are a student, worker, leader, business person, or a parent, you should do your best. Put your all into it. If you don't utilize and cultivate your talents and gifts, then both you and the world will have suffered a great loss. Take action today and give your very best. The world will no doubt be a better place if you do, because your best is good enough!

Common Sense, Not So Common

You either have common sense or you don't. If you have to be told what it is, chances are you don't have it! And if you do not have it, I do not think anyone can tell you how to get it. "All education and all the knowledge in the world can't help the poor soul who has no common sense... nothing astonishes men so much as common sense and plain dealing," said Ralph Waldo Emerson. He also said, "...common sense is genius dressed in its working clothes."

Common sense is that innate ability to know when, where, and how to act. It does not involve learning, it involves knowing instinctively the best decision to make under particular circumstances. It involves thinking first and then responding.

In the great book The Death of Common Sense, Philip K. Howard explains how our legal system has lost its way and often does not perform with common sense. While at times 'the system' and people do not behave with common sense, each of us can. So remember every day to use your common sense.

Character is Priceless

Character is your basic being, your attitude, standards, ideals, what you think and what you feel inside. You cannot really quantify it, but you know what kind of character you possess. John Wooden, college basketball's most revered coach, said, "Be more concerned with your character than your reputation, because your character is what you really are, while your reputation is merely what others think you are."

Your reputation is precious, but your character is priceless. Theodore Roosevelt said, "I care not what others think of what I do, but I care very much about what I think of what I do." That is character!

"Mental toughness is essential to success. Its qualities are sacrifice and self-denial. Also, most importantly it is combined with a perfectly disciplined will that refuses to give in. It's a state of mind – you could call it character in action," said Vince Lombardi.

Take action today; build a character that allows you to live a life of which you are proud. Forget about what others think, because character cares less about that. Character and success are not the same, but the former can only enhance the latter. Live a life of great character and live your best life!

Communication is Listening and Talking

Lisa Kirk said, "A gossip is one who talks to you about others... a bore is one who talks to you about himself... and a brilliant conversationalist is one who talks to you about yourself." We want to impress other people with our thoughts, knowledge, and expertise. We are so eager to solve other people's problems and to hear ourselves talk that we spend far too little time listening.

Successful people tend to be good listeners. They know they will rarely make a mistake when they talk less and listen more. As with all people skills, you can learn to be a good listener and to inspire others to speak freely.

What characteristics and attributes do successful people possess in this area? The answer is two-fold: they listen more than they talk and they get you to talk about yourself. They ask questions: How are you? What do you think about various current issues? How are your children?

When the conversation ends you think to yourself, 'Isn't that a wonderful, smart, pleasant, cheerful person?' They may well be, but you probably can't say for sure. They have made you feel wonderful, smart, pleasant, and cheerful by keeping their mouth shut and letting you talk. Listen more and talk less.

Courage First

It is easy to be ordinary, but it takes real courage to excel. It takes courage to stand by your convictions when all those around you have no convictions. It is easy to knock someone's dreams as ridiculous, but it takes courage to hold on to your dreams and encourage others in theirs in spite of the chatter around you.

It takes courage to live honestly and truthfully, in unbending accordance with those traits. All the greats, like Martin Luther King, Jr. and Nelson Mandela, who fought for the rights of people, had great courage. Bill Gates was mocked and ridiculed by the business community when he 'saw' a computer in everyone's home.

It takes courage to stick to your plan and the pursuit of your goals when you encounter severe obstacles. The secret of happiness is freedom, and the secret of freedom is courage. Winston Churchill said it best, "Courage is the first of the human qualities because it is the quality which guarantees all others."

Live a Life of Service

Service is the key to success in your career and life. Live to serve others and you will receive more than you could ever imagine. Your rewards in life are directly proportional to the service you provide others. First comes service, then come rewards. If you want greater rewards, provide greater service to others.

You cannot stand in front of a fireplace and say, "Give me heat, then I will put in the wood." Many businesses and people try the illogical approach of, 'give us your business, then we will provide you service'. The proper attitude is, 'allow us to first serve you so that we can then earn your confidence and your business'.

Zig Ziglar said, "You can get anything you want and need in life if you will just help enough other people get what they want and they need." You need to lose yourself completely in serving others, while doing something you love to do. Your happiness increases as your ability to serve to others increases. The harder you work at serving others, the happier you will be.

Implement with Strength

Proper implementation is the key to success in any endeavor. If you're a leader or manager, do not articulate a vision or mission unless you are prepared to implement it with overwhelming strength. Stay cool under fire, think big, act fast, and go for the big win! Elevate to mission status only those causes that are vital to your organization's success. You can't slay the dragon every day. Make sure that you choose your battles carefully.

Remain flexible. Pick your battles, but don't turn up your nose at opportunity. Even after you've settled on a winning strategy and tactics, be prepared to throw out the game plan if circumstances require it. When you're clear, consistent, and committed, you lend enormous strength to your organization. You also build your own credibility and authority, which is another plus for the organization.

Never stop articulating and living the message across your company's hierarchy. People follow people who live their message and lead by example. Think about it. If someone asks you to do something you know they haven't done, aren't you likely to think, "Why should I follow them, they've never done it before?"

"True courage is not the absence of fear, it's the mastery of fear."

-Mark Twain

Make the Investment

Your commitment to become an expert must be absolute—no deviations, no excuses. Pay any price. Go any distance. Spend any amount of time, and become the best at what you do; it will be the best investment you ever made! Discipline yourself. Give your talents and gifts plenty of preparation. Only then can you maximize your abilities.

Success basically equates to expertise. Becoming an expert requires a commitment of time, effort, and in some cases, money. Think of any expert teacher, mechanic, musician, athlete, business person, parent, friend or mate for that matter. Was their expertise and excellence achieved without expending time, effort and money where needed? Definitely not!

Your commitment and effort must come first. The success, rewards, and satisfaction will follow. It is what you bring to your job or relationship that's important and not what the job or relationship gives to you. You have control, not the job or other person. Success will come from paying the price; preparation, self-discipline, hard work, perseverance and faith.

We've all heard people say, "I would give anything to..." But the truth is they give very little, often nothing, to do those things. So what are you waiting for? To live your best life, pay the price for success and make the investment.

Live in the Solution

There was a time in my life when I chose to think about challenges and obstacles as just more of the "bad luck" I seemed to attract. Ever hear the expression 'when it rains it pours'? That was my constant mantra when others asked me how things were going. So what do you think I got more of? If you answered "rain" you're correct!

I learned that you're either living in the problem or you're living in the solution. Now, when I'm confronted with what I used to think was a negative situation, I use a different thought process. I force myself to replace those negative thoughts that creep in with positive thoughts about how I might solve the problem.

Sometimes I take out a notepad or my recorder and start jotting down or dictating possible solutions. At the same time, my thoughts are focused on the lessons I might learn from the situation so that I might profit from the experience in the future.

If you've guessed that it doesn't "rain" as much in my life as it used to, you're right. In fact, most days it's beautiful! Only occasionally do I get any rain, and it's good rain, the kind that makes living things grow!

Read the Right Books

We spend thousands of dollars a year on clothing, cosmetics, etc., to change or improve our outward appearance, but very little time or money to change our inward condition. Many people easily spend an hour a day doing nothing, but find every reason in the world not to spend a few minutes a day improving inwardly.

Since it is our thoughts that determine our life, you must focus on doing those things that will change your thoughts. Nothing is more effective at changing your thoughts than reading the right books.

Charlie Jones said, "You are today the same you'll be in five years from now, except for two things; the people you meet and the books you read. The people you meet can't always be with you, but what you read in books can remain with you a lifetime." Spend just 15 minutes every day before going to bed or upon rising, reading personal development books or biographies of people you admire.

Aldous Huxley observed, "Every person who knows how to read has it in his power to magnify himself, to multiply the ways in which he exists, to make his life full, significant, and interesting." Read the right books and live your very best life!

Cut People Some Slack

A long time ago someone told me something that completely changed my life. It seemed like they always cut people too much slack when they messed up or weren't nice. I was very confused because this person was very strong, and highly successful. He told me the reason he cut people slack when they were 'wrong' or 'not nice' was because he wanted them to do the same.

He explained, "I mess up from time to time and sometimes I can be unfair and not so nice. And when it happens, I hope that they will cut me a break and forgive me. I learned that if I want people to do that for me, then I have to do it with them." Wow! This blew me away. Ever since then I have done my best to forgive people and cut them lots of slack when they mess up, or do something I don't think is right or fair.

It has paid huge dividends for me in my relationships, as it will for you. So take action today by cutting people some slack. Forgive the people who have wronged you and move forward with a positive attitude. This will insure that you live your very best life!

You Receive What You Believe

Our expectations wield tremendous power and influence in our lives. We don't always get what we deserve in life, but we usually get no more than we expect; we receive what we believe. Unfortunately, this principle works as strongly in the negative as it does in the positive. Many people tend to expect the worst. They expect defeat, failure, and mediocrity. And they usually get what they expect.

But you can expect good things just as easily as you can expect the worst. It's possible to believe in more, to see yourself performing at higher levels in every area of life. When you encounter tough times, don't expect to stay there. Expect to come out of that trouble. When business gets a bit slow, don't assume you'll go bankrupt, and don't make plans for failure. Expect to come out and climb higher than before!

Low expectations will destroy our thinking, which in turn will hurt our circumstances. Quit expecting to fail and start believing that you are going to succeed. Focus on what you can do, not what you can't. Control the things you can control and don't focus on things you can do nothing about. When you do, you will live your very best life!

Live Now!

The great poet Piet Hein said, "Living is something you do now or never, which do you?" Too many people are waiting to 'live' by thinking think that life will become good 'one day'. Don't let fears, worries, obstacles or problems interfere with you living today!

Make today count, and enjoy every minute of it no matter what. When I was in the hospital for several months after a life threatening motorcycle accident, I had a choice. Do I focus on the fact that I am in severe pain and may never walk again; or do I focus on living as best as I can in that moment?

I chose to do my best to live each day with joy and hope, no matter what the doctor reports were telling me. I watched the TMC channel every day for the classic films. I really enjoyed seeing the old-time actors and actresses. I chose to get lost in those movies and I will never forget how much I enjoyed them.

So what are you waiting for? Living is something you do now or never, so don't waste another minute. Enjoy 'right now' and see yourself living your very best life!

Help Make the World a Better Place

Remember these three unfailing principles;

1) Our rewards in life will always match our service to others.
2) No one can become rich without enriching others.
3) Anyone who adds to prosperity must prosper in return.

Dale Carnegie said, "The rare individual who unselfishly tries to serve others has an enormous advantage, he has little competition."

Albert Schweitzer said, "I don't know what your destiny will be, but one thing I know: the only ones among you who will be really happy are those who have found how to serve." Albert Einstein warned, "Man is here for the sake of serving others - only!"

The greatest rewards and satisfaction I have received in my life come from knowing that in some small way I have served others. It is during those times that I feel most fulfilled and grateful. Give people your ears and listen, give them your heart and care, give them your forgiveness and support, and they will give you the world!

Find ways to do what John F Kennedy put to us: "Ask not what your country can do for you but what you can do for your country." Live your best life and live to enhance the lives of others.

Definitely Directed Thought

Most people spend more time planning their vacations than their lives. Most people spend more time thinking about unproductive issues than what's important in their life.

The power of "definitely directed thought" (the power of purpose) is why I love the story of John Goddard so much. At age 15, Goddard was inspired to create a list of 127 "life goals." By the time he was a "young seventy-something" Goddard had accomplished 109 of these, PLUS 300 others he set along the way!

He climbed the Matter Horn, Ararat, Kilimanjaro, Fiji, Rainer, and the Grand Tetons. He retraced Marco Polo's route through the Middle East, Asia, and China. He was the first man to explore the whole length of the world's longest river, the Nile.

He also boated down the Amazon, Congo and others. He flew 47 different types of aircraft, and set several civilian air-speed records including one at 1,500 miles an hour. He flew an F-106 to an altitude of 63,000 feet, making him the only civilian to pilot an aircraft that high, a record that he still holds.

How much would the quality of your life improve if you accomplished just one life goal in each of the next 10 years? You won't ever know if you don't start now.

"We become what we think about."

-Early Nightingale

Accept No Limits

You are not limited to the life you now live. Even if you've accepted your current situation, any time you're ready to go beyond the limitations currently in your life, you're capable of doing that by choosing different thoughts.

You don't believe it's true? George Dantzig was a college student who studied very hard and always late into the night. One morning he overslept, arriving 20 minutes late for class. He quickly copied the two math problems on the board, assuming they were the homework assignment.

It took him several days to work through the two problems, but finally he had a breakthrough and dropped the homework on the professor's desk. Later, on a Sunday morning, George was awakened by his excited professor. Since he was late for class, he did not hear the professor say that the two unsolvable equations on the board were mathematical teasers that even Einstein hadn't been able to answer.

George Dantzig, working without any thoughts of limitation, had solved not one, but two problems that had stumped mathematicians for thousands of years. Simply put, George solved the problems because he didn't know he couldn't. You have tremendous reservoirs of potential within you, and therefore you're capable of accomplishing anything you set your mind to do.

Someone Moved My Cheese

In one of the top-selling books of all time, "Who Moved My Cheese", Spencer Johnson points out that change is constant and we need to embrace it. Many people are upset because someone "moved their cheese." In other words, their jobs or other aspects of their life changed, and it negatively impacted them. They were not prepared for this change.

I hear people say, "Remember the good ol' days? Things were so much easier." My immediate concern is that these folks are not accepting (much less embracing) change. Only two things are constant in life, taxes and change. Did the record industry see digital downloading coming?

Everywhere we look things are changing. Our cheese is going to be moved. Will you get in the "maze" to look for new cheese, or will you wake up every day expecting your cheese to be there? When it's not, will you scream, "That's not fair what they did!"?

Embrace change, look ahead to what's coming, and do your best to prepare for it.

Believe It's Possible

You'll rarely attempt something that you don't believe is possible and you'll never give 100% to such an endeavor. David Schwartz said, "The size of your success is determined by the size of your belief."

I took to heart what Wayne Dyer wrote: "Work each day on your thoughts rather than concentrating on your behavior. It is your thinking that creates the feeling that you have and ultimately your actions as well." So I worked each day on my beliefs by constantly using written and verbal affirmations. The years since have been an incredible ride.

Roger Bannister was the first person to run a mile in under four minutes. Before he did it, it was generally believed that the human body was incapable of such a feat. But shortly after Bannister's accomplishment, many others did the same thing. Thousands have done so since, and today it's not uncommon for it to be done by a talented high-schooler. Did the human body change so that this could be done? No! But the human belief system did!

Remember Napoleon Hill's most famous 10 words, "Whatever your mind can conceive and believe, it can achieve." Just believing is a bold step towards living your very best life!

Soar With Eagles

Get around people who will build you up, not tear you down. Find a place where people will encourage and challenge you to be the best you can be. If you associate with successful people, their contagious enthusiasm will help you soar with the eagles.

I grew up in an environment where my friends were involved in things that put our futures at risk. Most of the friends I grew up with are either dead or in jail. The crowd I ran with had no dreams and found themselves in a bad place.

Fortunately for me, my mother moved me to Florida to live with my uncle. I ended up working for a company that had winners everywhere. The winning attitude rubbed off on me, and my life changed. To this day, I am surrounded by some of the most inspired, successful people on the planet, and I don't take these relationships for granted.

It's time for you to soar with the eagles rather than pecking around with the chickens. If you stay in an atmosphere of victory you can make this world a much better place.

Change

The other day I was with my daughter ordering an espresso macchiato. Unfortunately, the person taking my order did not understand what this coffee drink was and explained that she could not do it. I tried to explain to her how to make it and I could tell she was not happy about that. Needless to say, I did not get the drink I wanted.

After we walked away, my daughter asked me why it was so difficult for her to understand what I wanted. I explained to her that most people do not like change and this person did not want to get outside her box to do it. People who can adjust and make changes are people who get to experience life's diverse beauty. Robert Lewis Stevenson said this about change: "Where we are, it is but a stage on the way to somewhere else, and whatever we do, however well we do it, it is only a preparation to something else that shall be different."

I remember listening to one of my mentors telling me that the only change people like is the one that they control. He said no one wants change forced on them. But if you want to live a life of dreams, you must follow the advice of Henri Bergson, who said: "To exist is to change, to change is to mature, to mature is to go on to creating oneself endlessly."

Become Wealthy Today

An anonymous writer once said, "The real measure of a man's wealth is how much he would be worth if he lost all of his money." Wealth has nothing to do with accumulation of money. Wealth is knowledge, confidence and attitude. It is the security that comes from knowing that no matter what happens, you can always change your thinking, your beliefs, your actions, and your strategies, and still succeed.

Adopt this philosophy, 'You can take all of my cash, credit, assets – everything the world considers wealth. But I will always have the things that really count: my own natural resources, my supreme self-confidence, my time, my ability to communicate, my courage and my knowledge'. You do not have to have any money to be a success.

You can have lots of money and be poor in spirit, joy, happiness and confidence. So make a decision today that you will become wealthy in the ways that matter most. And by the way, the money will follow! It's a simple formula to live your very best life!

"The rare individual who unselfishly tries to serve others has an enormous advantage, he has little competition."

-Dale Carnegie

The Fountain of Youth

"Anyone who stops learning is old, whether at 20 or 80; anyone who keeps learning stays young," said Henry Ford. The most exciting, fun and interesting people are those who commit to a lifetime of learning. They have discovered the fountain of youth.

The most successful people set aside time for learning. First, start learning more about what you do for a living and how you can do it better. Get books from experts in your field and let them teach you.

Relationships require work, so learn more about yourself and others. Seek out information that teaches you to develop great relationships. Remember, if you are the smartest person in your circle, your circle is too small.

Get around people who know more than you do and learn from them. Ask them questions, pick their brains. Every successful person I know will share their expertise if you will simply ask. Don't forget to take notes!

Your Daily Agenda

The secret to success can be found in your daily agenda. If you make a few key decisions and manage them well every day, you will succeed. You won't change your life until you change something you do daily.

What you become depends on what you do today. How you live today prepares you for tomorrow. Are you preparing for success or failure? You can pay now and play later, or you can play now and pay later. Either way, you are going to pay.

Preparation breeds confidence. Brett Favre explained, "What I do is prepare myself until I know I can do what I have to do." Investing in today is like putting money in the bank. You're simply better prepared to meet life's challenges.

John Kotter, author of Leading Change said, "Most people don't lead their own lives, they accept their lives." Life is not a dress rehearsal. There's no second chance at today. Heed the words of British Prime Minister Benjamin Disraeli, who said, "The secret to success in life is for a man to be ready for his time when it comes."

Time is an equal opportunity employer, but we don't all 'employ' time equally. A point to consider if you want to live your very best life!

Master Your Fears

It's been said that we're born with only a few fears – like the fear of falling and the fear of loud noises. All other fear is learned along the way. Like the fear of failure, the fear of rejection – even the fear of success. I believe that our greatest enemy in life is fear, because fear keeps us from doing many things that would make our lives more complete and more enjoyable.

Doubt is the first cousin of fear and precedes it. We weren't born with doubt. Our habit of doubt has grown throughout our lives. If we dwell on a doubt and give into it, it then grows into fear. If most of our fears and all of our doubts are learned along the way, then we can unlearn them by becoming masters of our thoughts. Mark Twain said, "True courage is not the absence of fear, it's the mastery of fear."

The people who live the life of their dreams have just as many fears as those who live miserable, unfulfilled lives. They just have learned to master their fears instead of allowing their fears to master them. Master your fears and you will be living your very best life!

Formula for Success

James Allen said, "He conceives of, mentally builds up, an ideal condition of life; the vision of a wider liberty and a larger scope take possession of him; unrest urges him to action, and he utilizes all his spare time and means, small though they are, to the development of his latent powers and resources." Read these 52 words carefully and you will find the keys to success in any endeavor.

One study found that 94% of 3,000 people expressed no definite purpose for their lives. Is it any wonder that many people reach their twilight years feeling like life has passed them by? We have a choice to live our life on purpose or without a purpose. Life doesn't make distinctions, it simply rewards our choice.

Life's rewards are up to us, as explained in Think and Grow Rich: "I bargained with life for a penny, and life would pay no more, however I begged at evening when I counted my scanty store. For life is a just employer, he gives you what you ask, but once you have set the wages, why, you must bear the task. I worked for a menial's hire, only to learn, dismayed, that any wage I had asked of life, life would have willingly paid."

Persist Until it Rains

If I had to pick one character trait that I think is a "must-have" in order to be successful in any endeavor, it would be persistence. It seems to be the dominant trait in every super-successful individual I know. I believe it to be the one trait that any ordinary person can use to become extraordinary.

Napoleon Hill, who wrote Think and Grow Rich, devoted an entire chapter to persistence and said that the only difference between Henry Ford, Thomas Edison and everyone else was their persistence.

I love this story and hope it will encourage you as it has me over the years. There is a tribe in Africa that confounded all of the anthropologists. The tribe enjoyed a 100% success rate with its rain dance. In comparing this tribe to others who did not always experience success, the experts couldn't figure it out. They performed the same rituals, prayed the same incantations to the same gods, in the same costumes.

The successful tribe did one thing—only one thing—differently than the other tribes. They always danced until it rained! If your head is hanging low today, as mine has done on many days, I hope you'll find the encouragement to know that you only need to do one thing at this point: keep dancing until it rains!

Luck is When Preparedness Meets Opportunity

Earl Nightingale said it best: "Luck is what happens when preparedness meets opportunity." Opportunity is there all the time. How can you develop a good attitude so you can get 'lucky'? Treat every person you meet as the most important person on earth, because as far as they are concerned, they are.

Treat the members of your family as the very important people they really are, the most important in the world. Each morning, adopt a positive attitude. Notice how quickly it develops into a habit. Almost immediately, you will notice a change, and so will others. Irritations that once frustrated you will begin to disappear.

No one succeeds because they are 'lucky'. Everyone who succeeds does so because they have labored long and hard and in the most 'uncommon of hours'. Others will say they are lucky, but they know otherwise. Be prepared so when opportunity comes, you are ready to cash in and live your very best life.

Keep It Simple

Each day usually consists of a series of tasks. The success of a day depends upon the successful completion of most of those tasks. It's not so much the number of tasks you do but rather the quality of each separate action that counts.

Prioritizing those tasks is critical. Sort them into A, B, and C tasks. As are the ones you must get done today, B tasks are important but could get done in the next day or two, and C tasks are ones that can get done by the end of the week.

You'll find yourself increasing the number of tasks and performing them much more efficiently. You'll be amazed and very happy at the order this system brings into your life and the speed with which you'll be able to accomplish the things that need to get done.

All my life I've had a planner, a tool I use to organize my life and tasks that need to get done. This simple but tremendously effective method will take all of the confusion out of your life. You'll never find yourself running around in circles wondering what to do next.

100% Guaranteed Success

If you'll conscientiously go about the exercise I will outline, and concentrate on it every day, you'll find yourself becoming 'lucky' as the uninitiated call it. All sorts of wonderful things will begin happening in your life, and it will prove to you what a great attitude can mean. So here's the exercise: Treat every person with whom you come in contact as the most important person on earth. Do that for three excellent reasons:

1) As far as every person is concerned, he or she is the most important person on Earth.
2) That is the way human beings ought to treat each other.
3) By treating everyone this way, we begin to form an important habit.

There's nothing in the world that men, women and children want and need more than self-esteem. The feeling that they're important, that they're recognized, that they're needed, that they count and are respected. They'll give their love, their respect and their business to the person who fills this need.

We need to understand that how we get treated is based on how we treat others. The more we believe in others, the more others will believe in us. Live your very best life and understand that it's the law of sowing and reaping. It works 100% of the time.

"The greatest compliment that was ever paid me was when someone asked me what I thought, and then attended to my answer"

-Henry David Thoreau

Make Adjustments

"The pessimist complains about the wind. The optimist expects it to change. The leader adjusts the sails," said John Maxwell. The most successful and happy people are those who can adjust to circumstances. In his book The Art of Happiness, the Dalai Lama said this, "Even on an evolutionary scale, the species that have been most flexible, most adaptable, to environmental changes, have survived and thrived.

Every day we have to adjust. From the moment we get in our cars and head to work, we adjust our driving due to other drivers and road conditions. When you set out to succeed at something, things are not going to go perfectly as planned; you will need to make adjustments. If you set out in a boat and head into the ocean for a particular destination, there will be winds and natural currents that pull you off track. A boater is constantly adjusting the boat to keep on course.

The person who can be adaptable and adjust to all different kinds of people, circumstances and situations is the person who will live a more successful and happier life. So the next time things don't go your way, instead of getting upset, adjust. Instead of being negative, adjust. Instead of complaining, adjust. Keep adjusting and you will no doubt live your very best life!

Get Excited

I often see people waiting for something exciting to happen in their lives; they walk around joking about hitting the lottery one day. They go through the day in neutral, waiting for something great to happen. The problem with that is when you wait for exciting things to happen, life passes you by.

You must first get excited about your life, and what you are doing when you are doing it. This shift in thinking will cause your life to become more exciting, and all sorts of great things will happen. I remember one time listening to Zig Ziglar, who said, "Whatever you get excited about, will get excited about you." That always stuck with me. Life is way too short to go around worrying, depressed and complaining.

Get excited and enthusiastic about the life you have been given. Focus on what is right in your life, not what is wrong. Bring a new kind of enthusiasm to your work, being a parent, and the important relationships you are blessed to have. When you do, I promise you will be living your very best life!

The Half a Minute Rule

Within the first 30 seconds of a conversation, say something encouraging to a person. People everywhere need a good word or an uplifting compliment to fire their hopes and dreams. It takes very little effort to do, but it really lifts people up.

When most people meet others, they search for ways to make themselves look good. The key to the 30-Second Rule is reversing this practice. When you make contact with people, instead of focusing on yourself, search for ways to make them look good.

Every time you meet someone, pause to think about something encouraging you can tell them. What you can say is one of many things. You might thank someone for something they've done for you or for a friend. You might tell others about one of their accomplishments. You might praise them for a personal quality they exhibit. Or you might simply compliment their appearance.

The practice isn't complicated, but it does take some time, effort and discipline. The reward for practicing it is huge, because it really makes a positive impact on people and will at the same time help you to live your very best life.

Let People Know You Need Them

"The greatest compliment that was ever paid me was when someone asked me what I thought, and then attended to my answer," said Henry David Thoreau. John Maxwell said, "Leaders can become great only when they realize that they are the ones who need people." When the vision gets bigger than you, you only have two choices: give up on the vision or get help.

The day I realized that I could no longer do everything myself was a major step in my development as a person and a leader. I've always had vision, plenty of ideas, and vast amounts of energy. But when the vision got bigger than me, I really only had those two choices.

No matter how successful you are, no matter how important or accomplished, you do need people. That's why you need to let folks know that you cannot win without them. President Woodrow Wilson said, "We should not only use all the brains we have—but all that we can borrow." Enlist people's hands and hearts, too! Another president, Lyndon Johnson, was right when he said, "There are no problems we cannot solve together, and very few that we can solve by ourselves." So let people know you need them and you will be living your very best life.

Enjoy Every Moment On Earth

Few people admit to having enough time. However, we can all make better use of this precious resource. You never get time. You have to make time for the most important things. Think of time as an equal opportunity employer. You have exactly the same number of minutes and hours each day as everyone else. Successful people use each spare moment. The only way to make time is to use it wisely. Winners use their time well. Losers waste their time.

Your personal effectiveness will be determined by your ability to manage you time well. There is always enough time to do the important things and there is never enough to do everything. Identify your goals and make detailed plans for their accomplishment. Prioritize your activities. Focus on the vital few rather than the trivial many. Effective people do 'first things first', one thing at a time.

Never let the fear of time stand in your way. The time will pass anyway, whether or not you are making good use of it. What overwhelms us is thinking how hard and how time-consuming a task is going to be. Relax and enjoy every moment you are alive, and in doing so, you will be living your very best life.

Pass the Credit On to Others

"If each of us were to confess his most secret desire, the one that inspires all his plans, all his actions, he would say, "I want to be praised," said E.M. Cioran. The main reason people don't pass along credit to others is that they think it will somehow hurt them or lessen their value.

Many people are so insecure that they constantly feed their egos to compensate for it. But you simply cannot practice this method of winning with people if you can't set your ego aside. "An egotist is not a person who thinks too much of himself; it's someone who thinks too little of other people" wrote John C. Maxwell in 25 Ways to Win with People. Check your ego at the door.

If you want to give others credit, put your focus on others. What do they need? How will giving them credit make them feel? How will it enhance their performance? How will it motivate them to reach their potential? If you highlight their contributions, it makes them and you look good.

I love what H. Ross Perot said about passing on credit: "Reward employees while the sweat's still on their brow." Catch people while they are doing something good and you will end up living your very best life.

"The pessimist complains about the wind. The optimist expects it to change. The leader adjusts the sails."

-John Maxwell

Imitation or Original

Emotionally healthy people recognize and accept both their strengths and their limitations. They have a reasonably accurate picture of themselves and they like what they see. Consider your strong points. Be yourself. If you spend your life trying to emulate others, you are doomed to a life of frustration and despair. You can never achieve your best by imitating others.

Imitation is suicide. Envy is ignorance. If you develop your own powers, you have no need for imitation or envy. You can be as happy and successful as anyone if you build on the powers within you. In all walks of life, the most successful people are the risk takers.

Believe in your own ideas. Set out in pursuit of your own goals. Stand up for what you believe to be right. Take the risk of being different. When you find yourself, you will have a wonderful feeling that says, "This is it, I have found it, I am on the right road at last."

Remember, we become what we think about. We become what we choose to become, whether or not we realize it. Get into the habit of forming your own independent opinions through study, research and most importantly personal observation. Do not worry about what other people think or say. When you do this, you will be living your very best life.

Listen With Your Heart

"The most important thing on communication is to hear what isn't being said," said Peter Drucker. President Woodrow Wilson said, "The ear of the leader must ring with the voices of the people." If you are already a good listener, you are ahead of the game. All you have to do is 'read between the lines' for cues that will tell you how others feel. We all need to learn the skill of listening with our hearts.

Herb Cohen, often called the world's best negotiator, said, "Effective listening requires more than hearing the words transmitted. It demands that you find meaning and understanding in what is being said. After all, meanings are not in words, but in people."

In the sales profession, the best salesperson is not the best talker but the best listener. This enables them to be more empathetic and care for the person by helping them solve their problems and fill their needs.

Put other people first and focus on the individual, not just the ideas being expressed. If you view complaints or criticism as a personal attack, you will become defensive. Once you begin to protect yourself, you will care little about what others think or how they feel. So listen with your heart and live your very best life.

Generosity – It's Own Reward

It may be easy for people to find reasons not to give, or be generous. But it's just as easy to find reasons to give. When we are generous with our time, money, effort, and kindness, whether at work, home, or away, it comes back to us a hundredfold. I know this not because I read it in some book, but because I have seen it in my life and in the lives of so many others.

When we are generous with people, we give them the green light to be generous with others as well. When we are generous with our money, it always comes back with lots of interest. It is a biblical principle that works 100% of the time: "As you sow, so it shall be given back to you ... good measure, pressed down, shaken together and running over."

When we are generous with our time and resources with our family, it comes back a hundredfold. When we are generous with those we call our friends, it comes back a hundredfold. When we are generous in our work and we give more than what is expected, we have a right to expect a greater return than someone who does not give with the same measure.

Be generous in all that you do, and you will surely live your very best life!

Self—Esteem and Confidence

"Of all the judgments that we pass in life, none is as important as the ones we pass on ourselves, for that judgment touches the very center of our existence," said Nathaniel Brandon. Esteem means "to appreciate the worth of." So self-esteem means to appreciate ourselves. It's confidence in our basic ability to cope with the challenges and opportunities of life, trust our own mind and judgment and instill in ourselves the belief and feeling that we are worthy of happiness.

Self-esteem is not derived from the things you do, the objects you possess, or what other people think of you. Your own happiness and self-esteem are what you determine them to be. They're inside of you, not outside. It's amazing how many people go through life without recognizing that their feelings toward other people are largely determined by their feelings toward themselves.

If you're not comfortable with yourself, you can't be comfortable with others. If you don't respect yourself, you can't respect others. If you don't love yourself, you will not be able to love others. You can't give that which you don't possess. So let's esteem ourselves and live our very best life!

Get in Synch

Have you ever met a person who said one thing and did another? One minute they believe their dreams will come to pass, the next minute they act like they'll never get where they want to be. What they haven't realized is their actions aren't in sync with their faith. We need our words, actions, and beliefs to work in tandem. Putting the right actions behind your faith and thoughts will give you a winning advantage.

What are you hoping for? You can put some action behind your hopes by talking and behaving with a positive end in view. When you do, you're not just thinking and believing—you're expecting!

If you don't like your situation, choose to put some action behind your thoughts and desires. Start today with announcements like, "I am a success. Whatever I touch prospers. My best days are in front of me." Speak your faith with confidence, then act with confidence! As you line up your words with your actions, your faith and confidence will grow stronger. You'll find peace knowing you're one day closer to seeing your dreams come to pass!

Albert Was Right

Albert Einstein gave us a lot of great quotes. Two favorites are: "You cannot solve a problem with the same mindset that created it." And, "The definition of insanity is doing the same thing over and over, and expecting different results." I think we all know the truth of these phrases.

How many of you have seen the same, tired ideas applied to recurring problems? Without knowing the specifics, or trying to be negative, I'm sure most failed. The truth is that if you don't change your mindset, you will try the same things over and over. Why? Because a limited mindset results in the perception of limited choices.

I love the story of the truck that got lodged in a tunnel. Attempt after attempt was made to dislodge the truck with various tow vehicles. Suddenly, a young responder suggested taking the air out of the tires. Once done, there was enough clearance to remove the truck. People commented that no one was thinking in three dimensions before his suggestion.

My friends, let's try to be that young responder. It's not easy to change our thinking and methods, or to suggest that others do so as well; but the results can be spectacular. Cultivate an open mindset and you'll live your best life.

Don't Interrupt Others

Years ago I realized how often I interrupted others and/or finished their sentences. Shortly thereafter, I also realized how destructive this habit was, not only to the respect and love I received from others but also for the tremendous amount of energy it takes to try to be in two heads at once! Think about that for a moment. When you hurry someone along, interrupt someone, or finish his or her sentence, you have to keep track not only of your own thoughts but of those of the person you are interrupting as well.

This tendency encourages both parties to speed up their speech and their thinking. This, in turn, makes both people nervous, irritable, and annoyed. It's downright exhausting. It's also the cause of many arguments, because if there is one thing almost everyone resents, it's someone who doesn't listen to what they are saying. And how can you really listen to what the person is saying when you are speaking for that person?

Catch yourself doing that and remind yourself to be patient and wait. Hold your tongue and listen. At first it will be uncomfortable, but you will feel good and then do it again and again until it becomes habit. Do this and you will be living your very best life for sure!

Say "Thank You" to Someone Every Day

This simple strategy, which may take only a few seconds to complete, has long been one of the most important habits I have ever engaged in. I try to remember to start my day thinking of someone to thank. To me, gratitude and inner peace go hand in hand. The more genuinely grateful I feel for the gift of my life, the more peaceful I feel.

Gratitude, then, is worthy of a little practice. If you're anything like me, you probably have many people in your life to feel grateful for: friends, family members, people from your past, teachers, gurus, people from work, someone who gave you a break, as well as countless others. You may want to thank a higher power for the gift of life itself, or for the beauty of nature.

As you think of people to be grateful for, remember that it can by anyone: someone who allowed you to merge into traffic, someone who held the door open for you, or a physician who saved your life. The point is to gear your attention toward gratitude, preferably first thing in the morning. I learned a long time ago that it's easy to allow my mind to slip into various forms of negativity. When I do, the first thing that leaves me is my sense of gratitude. I begin to take people in my life for granted, and the love that I often feel is replaced with resentment and frustration.

What this exercise reminds me to do is to focus on the good in my life. So take time to say thank you to someone in your life and let's live our very best lives!

"Genius is 1% inspiration and 99% perspiration."

-Thomas Edison

Find Strength Through Adversity

Living your best life is downright difficult sometimes. Many people give up far too easily when things don't go their way, or when faced with adversity. Instead of persevering, they get all bent out of shape. They become discouraged, which is understandable, especially when struggling with a problem or a weakness for a long time. It's not unusual to come to a place where we acquiesce.

You have to be more determined than that. You must do your best to find strength through adversity. Your circumstances in life may occasionally knock you down. The good news is that you don't have to stay down. Even if you can't see a means for getting up in the physical world, start by getting up on the inside. Have that victor's attitude and mentality. Stay with an attitude of faith and hope.

Every adversity carries a seed of equivalent opportunity. Setbacks will make you stronger if you see them that way. It may be hard, but such is life and it's not fair at times. Don't use these times to whine, use them to win! Never give up and you will be living your very best life!

Ask! Ask! Ask!

"You've got to ask. Asking is, in my opinion, the world's most powerful and neglected secret to success and happiness," said Percy Ross. History is filled with examples of incredible riches and astounding benefits people have received by simply asking for them. Yet surprisingly, asking—one of the most powerful success principles—is still a challenge that holds most people back.

If you're not afraid to ask anybody for anything, then you'll succeed on a grand scale. But if you are like most people, you may be holding yourself back by not asking for the: information, assistance, support, money, and time you need to fulfill your vision and make your dreams come true.

Why are people so afraid to ask? They're afraid of looking needy, looking foolish and looking stupid. But mostly they're afraid of rejection. They're afraid of hearing the word no. The sad thing is that they're actually rejecting themselves in advance.

Follow these simple steps. One, ask as if you expect to get it. Two, assume you can have whatever it is you're asking for. Three, ask someone who can give it to you. Four, be clear and specific. Five, ask repeatedly. If at first you don't succeed try again. Keep asking!

Be a Person of Integrity

The goal is to become a person of integrity, a person of honor, a person who is trustworthy. A person of integrity is open and honest and true to his word. They don't have any hidden agendas or ulterior motives. They don't need legal contracts to force fulfillment of their commitments. People of integrity are the same in private as they are in public. They do what's right whether or not anybody is watching.

If you don't have integrity, you'll never reach your highest potential. Integrity is the foundation on which a truly successful life is built. Every time you compromise your integrity, every time you're less than honest, you cause a slight crack in your foundation. If you continue compromising, that foundation will never be able to hold up the dreams and goals you are pursuing.

You'll never have lasting prosperity without integrity. You may enjoy some temporary success, but you'll never see the best that's in store for you unless you take the high road and make more excellent choices. There's no limit to what you can obtain or accomplish, if you decide to live with integrity.

Face What Isn't Working

"Our lives improve only when we take chances – and the first and most difficult risk we can take is to be honest with ourselves," said Walter Anderson, editor of Parade Magazine.

If you're going to become more successful, get out of denial and face what isn't working in your life. Do you defend or ignore a hostile and toxic work environment? Do you make excuses for your bad marriage? Are you in denial about your lack of energy, weight, health or level of physical fitness?

Are you failing to acknowledge that sales have been on a downward trend for the last quarter? Are you putting off confronting an employee who's not delivering at an acceptable standard of performance? Successful people face these circumstances squarely, heed the warning signs, and take appropriate action, no matter how uncomfortable or challenging it might be.

To face what's not working in your life usually means you're going to have to do something uncomfortable. It means you might have to exercise more self-discipline, confront somebody, risk not being liked, ask for what you want, demand respect instead of settling for an abusive relationship, or maybe even quit your job. Because you don't want to do these uncomfortable things, you'll often defend tolerating a situation that doesn't work.

Be willing to look at and take action on what is not working.

Make Nutrition a Priority

Admit it; you want to look better naked. Your first step to reaching that goal is adapting the way you eat to fit a healthy lifestyle. Some people like to call adapting the way you eat a diet. I don't. That's because it's the way you should be eating whether you're overweight, underweight, or a healthy weight. A diet is a fad, and it's not sustainable for the rest of your life. On a diet you'll still want to indulge in foods that don't add fuel to your body, but do add inches to your waistline. If you cut those foods, you'll probably be pretty miserable.

So stop the cycle. Instead of focusing on what you can and can't eat, focus on what provides your body with nutrition. Challenge yourself to include lean proteins, complex carbohydrates, and healthy fats together in every meal.

Making adjustments in the way you eat doesn't mean you have to go without your favorite junk food forever. It means that most of your meals and snacks will taste good and be good for you. Eating well will bolster your immune system, help your body to repair damaged cells, lower your risk of heart disease, cancer, and osteoporosis, and even increase your longevity. Make nutrition a priority and you'll live your very best life.

Let the Love Flow from You

When you've been hurt, it's hard to let down your guard and allow the love to flow from you unfettered. We've all been hurt. It's how you choose to react that matters. When you permit feelings of fear, jealousy, angst, the need to control, or resentment to take charge, it's easy to become bitter and defensive. By doing so, you erect barriers that prevent you from finding true love.

We often attract what we put out. That means if you approach love in a negative way, you're more likely to find someone who is bitter, defensive, resentful, or jealous. Try instead to let go of your hurt and to take steps to heal yourself in healthy ways. Do all of those things for yourself that your last partner didn't. Write about the experience in a journal to allow yourself to process all of your feelings. Look within yourself to see where you can improve as a partner.

Be a force of love, support, joy, and peace. Believe in the power of love and that you will find someone who treats you as you deserve. You'll be impressed at how positive thoughts and actions will bring you what you want. Let love flow from you and live your very best life.

"Whatever your mind can conceive and believe, it can achieve."

-Napoleon Hill

Use the Right Language

You may be surprised, but the language you use can have a profound impact on whether you'll manifest a positive or negative outcome. If you're skeptical about the power of manifestation, just think of it as setting your intentions.

For example, pretend you're about to go onstage and give a speech in front of hundreds of people. Like most people, you'd probably have a few butterflies! If you were to think, "I'm so nervous, I'm going to forget what I'm saying and they're all going to laugh at me," you're likely to make yourself even more anxious, and you might even forget your speech.

But if you were to tell yourself, "Hey, this is pretty exciting. I get to go up there and share my views with all of these people," then you're going to psych yourself up. You stand a better chance of delivering a powerful presentation.

It's important to be mindful of the language you use in all areas of your life. By empowering yourself with uplifting language and setting your intentions to get a new job, move to a new place, find a great partner, or do better in your line of work, you'll subconsciously make choices that put you on the path to deeper happiness.

Smile More Often

The more often you smile, the happier you'll be. And you might even live longer! A recent study that examined the smiles of retired baseball players found that those who smiled big lived longer than those who didn't.

Perhaps that's because the mere act of smiling can make you feel happy and happier people tend to live longer than those wrought with angst and frustration. If you're in a negative mood, you can improve it just by smiling! That's because when you activate the smile muscles, you're telling your brain that you're happy. And this creates a positive feedback loop within your body.

Though it might not be easy at first and you might not feel like smiling, smiling for a count of 10 and then deepening the smile and holding it can actually shift your mood in a positive direction, even if you're faking it. My mother taught me to fake it till you make it!

In addition, when you smile, you attract other positive people to you. It's a great cycle; smile at someone and he or she might smile back, which will make you feel good and want to smile more.

So smile more often and you will get happier and healthier.

Life (Time) Management

Make a list of all the projects you have or want to accomplish. Pick the one that is most important, and begin working on it. Do a little bit each day. Before you know it, time will have passed and you will have completed your project. With it, you will have achieved a new competence, a new satisfaction, and ultimate success in your efforts.

There is an unbelievably positive cumulative effect of a little time spent well each day. Here are some principles for proper time management: commit to using your time wisely and effectively; set aside time each day for thinking, reflecting, and planning; implement a 'do it now' philosophy; develop a sense of urgency for accomplishment. Think on paper; write down your plans, ideas and responsibilities.

Prioritize the items on your list in their order of importance. Work from that list. Concentrate on one thing at a time. Stick with that one thing until it is completed. If it is not on the list, do not do it.

Discipline yourself to get up each day and focus on your most important job first; even though you might not feel like it. I have learned to do what I need to do, not what I feel like doing.

Get Connected

We all talk, but are we connecting? As a public speaker I discovered very early that just because I was excited by the subject matter, that did not mean that people were listening, much less connecting with my message. We have all heard great communicators who can inspire people to reach higher. We have listened to others where we found ourselves counting down the minutes to when they would finish.

So how do we connect with others? The first step is to do your best to understand the other person and/or audience first, if you speak to many. "Seek First To Understand, Then To Be Understood," said Stephen Covey in The 7 Habits of Highly Successful People. "Connecting is the ability to identify with people and relate to them in a way that increases your influence with them," said leadership expert John Maxwell.

The ability to communicate and connect with others is a major determining factor in reaching your potential. It is a skill that anyone can learn. Do more listening than talking, ask questions, and as Steven Covey teaches, "Seek first to understand, then to be understood."

Friends — Who Are They?

It is very important to differentiate between friends and acquaintances. Acquaintances are people we know. Friends are people we enjoy, are completely comfortable with, can talk to, and trust implicitly. It has been said that in life we will have many acquaintances, but very few friends. True, loyal, and lasting friends are exceedingly rare and wonderful.

If you are fortunate to have friends, cherish and nurture them. The natural tendency in relationships is toward eroding attentiveness and sensitivity. Do not ignore or neglect your friends. Work hard to preserve them. Give them all the energy you have. Be alert to making new friends. No one has too many friends. Making new friends is both interesting and rewarding, because new friends bring change and excitement into your life.

If you tend to be shy and bashful, if you feel uncomfortable around new people, remember the stranger you are reluctant to meet may be just as reluctant to meet you.

Some words of caution: do not associate with individuals who are chronic complainers, whiners, or have negative attitudes. Cultivate friendships with positive, enthusiastic, intelligent, and cheerful people. Choose your friends carefully. Be sure you associate with the kind of people you would most like to resemble.

Do this and live your best life, with great friends to share it.

Settling For Average

Columnist Maureen Dowd said, "The minute you settle for less than you deserve, you get even less than you settle for." Dreams require a person to stretch, to go beyond average. You can't reach for a dream and remain safely mediocre at the same time. The two are incompatible.

When we are too uninspired to dream, when we settle for average, we may be tempted to blame it on others, on our circumstances, or on the system. But the truth is that mediocrity is always a personal choice.

Author Kenneth Hildebrand expressed the negative effect of such an existence: "The poorest of all men is not the one without a nickel to his name. He is the fellow without a dream... he is like a great ship made for the mighty ocean but trying to navigate in a millpond. ...He has no far port to reach, no lifting horizon, no precious cargo to carry. His hours are absorbed in the routine and petty tyrannies. Small wonder if he gets dissatisfied, quarrelsome and "fed up". One of life's greatest tragedies is a person with a 10-by-12 capacity and a two-by-four soul."

Build a Personal Sanctuary

When you step into your home, you want to feel it is reaching out and comforting you after a long day of work. But perhaps you live with a messy roommate, or your kids leave their toys strewn about, or you're just not the most organized individual.

So you open the door to find the sink full of dishes, laundry to be done, your roommate lounging on the couch with her feet on your nice coffee table… you get the point. Before you lose your mind, take control of what you can. If it's just your bedroom you have domain over, transform it into a sanctuary.

Of course, if you can work your magic on the whole house, even better. But no matter what, you'll need a room to which you can escape for relaxation. To take a room from four walls to sanctuary, first clean out the clutter. Paint the rooms in colors that are comforting to you. Put lights on dimmers so they're not so intense. Add candles to be lit at night to an even softer glow to the atmosphere.

You may even want to grab some flowers to add a nice smell to the house. Turning your home into a sanctuary will calm and relax you after a full day out and create a warm feeling so that every time you come home, you will be looking forward to it.

Worry – A Waste Of Time

Worrying can't do you any good. It can be very harmful mentally, emotionally, psychologically and physically. Too many people are consumed by needless worry. They allow worries to control their lives, preventing them from enjoying a positive, happy, productive, and fulfilling life.

Consider the following as reliable estimates of what people worry about: Things that haven't happened yet and probably never will: 40%. Things from the past that cannot be changed by all the worry in the world: 30%. Needless worries about your health: 12%. Petty, insignificant things that are not worth worrying about: 10%. Legitimate situations that deserve your attention and concern: 8%.

Focus your energies on the 8%. Devote yourself to events that are significant and over which you can determine the solutions and outcomes. The tragedy of many people's lives is that worry robs them of the sense that they are competent to cope with life's challenges and deserve happiness.

They are so consumed and preoccupied by worry that they don't trust their own thoughts, instincts, and abilities. They don't feel capable of asserting their own legitimate interests and needs. Remember that just about all of your concerns solve themselves one way or another.

"Life is a precious gift, but we realize this only when we give it too others."

-Pope Francis

Live Completely

French essayist Michel Eyquem de Montaigne wrote, "The value of life lies not in the length of days, but in the use we make of them; a man may live long yet live very little." The truth is that you can spend your life any way you want, but you can spend it only once. Becoming a big-picture thinker can help you to live with wholeness, to live a very fulfilling life.

People who see the big picture expand their experience because they expand their world. As a result, they accomplish more than narrow-minded people and they experience fewer unwanted surprises, too, because they are more likely to see the many components involved in any given situation: issues, people, relationships, timing and values. They are also, therefore, usually more tolerant of other people and their thinking.

Few people want to be closed-minded. No one sets out to be that way. We slowly and subtly begin to accept less than our best. We stop asking questions, we stop learning, and a closed mind follows. No one plans it, it just happens if you don't think and get around people who will inspire you to think.

So make it a point to live fully and completely in each day, empty your gas tank and while you sleep it will be filled up again for the next day.

Tell The Truth, Even If It's Hard To Do

One way to reduce the stress in your life is to tell the truth. It feels good to be honest, though not brutally so, to those around you. Telling the truth builds trust between partners, family, and friends and leads to longer-lasting, more meaningful relationships.

Though sometimes telling the truth can be difficult to do, especially if you've done something you're not proud of, it prevents you from having to deal with the guilt of lying and potential need to create more lies to cover up that one lie.

In addition to telling the truth, speaking up with the truth is an important part of being a better friend and partner. If someone you care about in your life is doing something that is harmful to herself or himself, try to be strong enough to approach that person and to speak honestly of the situation.

Though you might need the help of other friends and family members to do this, your loved one is likely to appreciate your concern in the long run. Tell the truth even if it's hard to do.

Become More Tolerant of Others

Letting go of your habit of judging others for having a different lifestyle then you will lift a burden off of your shoulders. Dislike of another person can come from what your parents or the society in which you were raised taught you. You believed them either because you were too young to have a reason to disagree or because you wanted to fit in.

Now you're old enough to revisit your beliefs to see if and why they still hold true for you. Challenge yourself to find holes in your intolerant beliefs and to be open-minded to hearing the opinions of someone who you see as different from yourself. You'll probably find the two of you have more in common than you thought.

As you work to become more tolerant and accepting of others and their beliefs, you will become smarter because you'll learn about other ways of life. You'll become happier because you will no longer walk around holding onto anger. Being open minded to having friends who differ from you in their race, religion, political beliefs, sexual orientation, and other ways can enrich your own life because it allows you the opportunity to see things from another's point of view.

Do the Impossible

"Nothing is so embarrassing as watching someone do something that you said could not be done," said Sam Ewing. People who are possibility thinkers are capable of accomplishing tasks that seem impossible because they believe in solutions. When you believe you can do something difficult—and you succeed—many doors open for you. When George Lucas succeeded in making Star Wars, despite those who said the special effects he wanted hadn't ever been done and couldn't be done, many other possibilities opened up to him.

Industrial Light and Magic, the company he created to produce those "impossible" special effects, became a source of revenue to help underwrite his other projects. It also attracted new, exciting people into his life. If you want to achieve big things, you need to see the possibilities. If you are a leader and you do this, you will be teaching others how to do the same, and they too will achieve things that they would otherwise not have achieved.

No matter what you do, possibility thinking can help you broaden your horizons and dream bigger dreams. Professor David J. Schwartz believes, "Big thinkers are specialists in creating positive forward looking, optimistic pictures in their own minds and in the minds of others."

Saved by Criticism

Norman Vincent Peale said, "The trouble with most of us is that we would rather be ruined by praise than saved by criticism." Still, after 35 years in business, I am being 'saved by criticism'. Recently I traveled to several other operations within my company to learn from the very best leaders.

They showed me what they were doing to have such great success. Now I have been in that business for 35 years, so you would think I would be the one offering them advice. Not the case! I listened to and have implemented much of what they are doing because I would rather be saved by criticism then ruined by praise.

So if you would like to see some growth and improvements in your life, talk with someone you trust. If you don't have someone like that, go to a professional counselor or life coach and take their advice one day at a time.

The same is true in relationships. Use the criticism you receive to make you better, not bitter. Even if people are criticizing you to make themselves feel better, use it to make yourself better.

Keep Hope Alive

Writer Mark Twain warned: "Keep away from people who try to belittle your ambitions. Small people always do that, but the really great make you feel that you, too, can become great." How do most people feel when they're around you? Do they feel small and insignificant, or do they believe in themselves and have hope about what they can become?

The key to how you treat people lies in how you think about them. It's a matter of attitude. How you act reveals what you believe. Johann Wolfgang von Goethe, emphasized, "Treat a man as he appears to be and you make him worse. But treat a man as if he already were what he potentially could be, and you make him what he should be."

Napoleon Bonaparte had it right: "A leader is a dealer in hope." Hope is perhaps the greatest gift you can give others as the result of nurturing because even if their sense of self is weak and they fail to see their own significance, they still have a reason to keep trying and striving to reach their potential in the future.

"My general attitude to life is to enjoy every minute of every day. I never do anything with a feeling of, 'Oh God, I've got to do this today.'

-Richard Branson

Never Outshine the Master

"Always make those above you feel comfortably superior. In your desire to please and impress them, don't not go too far in displaying your talents or you might accomplish the opposite - inspire fear and insecurity. Make your masters appear more brilliant than they are and you will attain the heights of power," said Robert Green.

Everyone has insecurities. When you show yourself in the world and display your talents, you naturally stir up all kinds of resentment, envy, and other manifestations of insecurity. You should expect this, but you cannot spend your life worrying about the feelings of others. With those above you, however, you must take a different approach: When it comes to power, outshining the master is perhaps the worst mistake of all.

Do not fool yourself into thinking that life has changed much since the days of Louis XIV and the Medicis. Those who attain high standing like kings and queens want to feel secure in their positions, and superior to those around them in intelligence, wit, and charm. It is a deadly but common misperception to believe that in displaying and flaunting your gifts and talents, you are winning the master's affection.

So quietly and wisely go about respecting the masters and they will give you the keys to the kingdom.

Stop Holding Grudges

Life lets us down. People we count on disappoint us; others transgress against us. A financial fortune is lost overnight, a healthy body is broken in an instant like mine was. When misfortune strikes, some people generate enormous resentment against others or against life in general; they are determined to extract some measure for what they have lost. Others accept their fate and go on to make the best of life—making lemonade out of lemons. You can free yourself of grudges.

Recognize that the grudge is weighing you down and holding you back. Even if you recapture what you've lost, you'll only regain the status quo. Use your precious time, instead, to grow and to advance. Don't allow misfortune to turn you into an entitlement seeker. Instead of focusing on your rights and what you have coming to you, aim for the higher things in life. Help others out of fixes like yours, accomplish an extraordinary feat, acquire knowledge and leave behind a meaningful legacy.

Visualize the troubling event. Reduce the size of the picture by moving it away from you. Make it as small as you can. Each time you do this, start with a smaller picture, and you'll eventually be free from it. Holding grudges does not affect the person you are holding it against; it holds you in bondage and keeps you from living your best life.

Slow Down and Enjoy Your Life

I don't want to confuse anybody by telling you to not dream big dreams and go after them with all you've got, but at the same time I want you and me to enjoy the journey.

One of the greatest running backs ever, Emmitt Smith, said that when he went home that night with his Super Bowl ring and trophy for some reason it didn't feel like he thought it would.

He went on to say that it was then that he realized that it was about the journey; it was about enjoying every day that he played the game and the people he played it with.

An old saying comes to mind: "stop and smell the roses."

Don't come to the end of your life chasing all those big dreams and accumulating all that wealth, only to find you have no one to love or who loves you, no friends or family to celebrate the great life that we were blessed to live.

The other day I found myself in a traffic jam and instead of getting upset I said to myself, it's all good, you're probably being protected from something tragic so just relax and enjoy the music and the surroundings.

The older I get the more I realize how short and precious life really is. Live each day to the full and be grateful for these are the real secrets to enjoying your life.

Acknowledgments

There were shoulders of many people I have stood upon, and continue to stand upon, along with a new group of people I know I will add to the growing list of people who have impacted my life.

I want to thank all of you from the bottom of my heart for the love and wisdom you shared with me at a time in my life when it meant everything to me. President Bill Clinton decided after meeting John F. Kennedy that he would one day be president.

He was so inspired by that one encounter, his life moved in an entirely different direction. To all of you on this list, my life moved in a new direction and so from the bottom of my heart I want to thank you!

And to the Creator of it all, God in heaven. Thank you for all you have done in my life and all that you are about to do. I pray that this body of work will reach the hearts and minds of all who read the pages and that their lives are better for doing it.

Russell Sangudolce - met after I was sleeping on the beaches and trained me how to sell insurance.

Andrew Wik - took me in off the beaches and gave me a home where I could take the time to learn my craft.

Dewy Britton - the first motivational speaker I ever heard at Bankers Life, the second insurance company I worked for.

Art Williams - the founder of Primerica - he taught me how to recruit people into the insurance business.

Lenny Furer - trained me at American Income Life and then made me his partner in my first insurance agency in New Jersey.

Bernard Rapoport - was a father to me and helped me become a man. Taught me how to dream big and never quit!

Marc Zipper - a friend closer than a brother. Without him, life would not be the same. He is my closest confidant/friend.

Steven Covey - prolific thinker and father of The 7 Habits of Highly Effective People. Listened endlessly.

Earl Nightingale - the father of positive thinking and personal growth. I listened to his tapes hundreds of times.

Tom Hopkins - the greatest sales trainer ever! Bought his most exclusive library of tapes and grew my business!

Brian Tracy - leadership and sales trainer to whom I have listened and shared his work, personally spent time with.

Zig Ziglar - got to spend some good time with him on several occasions. A profound and iconic man, he will be missed.

John Maxwell - met and worked with him several times and have his work as a staple part of our training.

BELIEVE IN YOURSELF
LIVE YOUR BEST LIFE
NURTURE YOUR BODY, MIND AND SPIRIT
LISTEN MORE, TALK LESS
PERSIST
TAKE LESS, GIVE MORE
READ AND GROW